Mother of Hollywood

by
Rev. Luminita Dragu

DORRANCE
PUBLISHING CO
EST. 1920
PITTSBURGH, PENNSYLVANIA 15238

Dorrance Publishing Co
585 Alpha Drive
Suite 103
Pittsburgh, PA 15238
Visit our website at www.dorrancebookstore.com

ISBN: 978-1-6480-4506-6
eISBN: 978-1-6480-4485-4

SALVATION TO THE GENTILES MINISTRY

Hollywood

The Word

Mother of Hollywood: Book

When I began writing this book to Hollywood, I did not know what I was getting into. I started to write biographies of Hollywood Stars and was awestruck at some of their huge successes. So I bring certain stars; of course, I could not bring them all in this book, or even the ones I wrote about, I could not write everything about their successes because it is too much. I would have to write a book on each one of them, and this is not feasible. Their achievements are overwhelming, including their earning and net worth. They work very hard, even for others like humanitarian work or charitable work. They invest their time and their lives into other people's lives and adversities through humanitarian work, charitable work. They are worthy of respect and recognition.

Being a Pastor, also a Pastor to Hollywood, I observe and deal with the sins of Hollywood. I give them Biblical counsel and mentor them, and they are receptive to my ministering to them. I minister to them many times from the point of their adversity. Further, I observe dangers surrounding the Hollywood Stars and intervene by alerting them of the dangers.

This book is written to Hollywood and contains instructions, teachings, and admonitions in the Word. It also contains cases and comments into the Me Too Movement, which I observe through visions. Triumphs and achievements of stars and their challenges and adversities. I am the Spiritual Mother of Hollywood and have written to the stars and mentored them for the past twelve plus years. I write into their issues of life because I observe their lives through visions through the Holy Spirit.

My journey with Hollywood began about twenty-five years ago when I began interceding in prayer on behalf of stars for their salvation and for their well-being. As the years progressed, I began to have visions into their private lives, including visions of their illnesses, weight issues, adultery, divorce, dangers such as car accidents from alcohol consumption or drugs, visions of fatal drug overdoses, visions of impending murder or robbery or rape, crimes of Hollywood and crimes against Hollywood. I startle stars with my knowledge into their private lives, but even so I continue to intervene on their behalf.

My calling is to convert Hollywood, to bring them to the knowledge of God and His Son Jesus Christ, to bring them to a life of holiness, so they can be a beacon of light in this nation and to this lost world. May Hollywood grow and mature in God's Word for, "Faith comes by hearing and hearing by the Word of God" Romans 10:17. "God, who is rich in mercy, for His great love where with He loved us, even when we were dead in our sins, God quickened us together with Christ (by grace we are saved). And has raised us up together and made us sit together in heavenly places in Christ Jesus, that in the ages to come, He might show the exceeding riches of His grace in His kindness toward us through Christ Jesus, for by grace are ye saved through faith, and that not of yourselves; it is the gift of God; not of works lest any man should boast. For we are His workmanship, created in Christ Jesus unto good works, which God has before ordained that we should walk in them," Ephesians 2:4-10.

God the Father

"Blessed be the God and Father of our Lord Jesus Christ, who has blessed us with all spiritual blessings in heavenly places in Christ; according as He has chosen us in Him before the foundation of the world, that we should be holy and without blame before Him in love, having predestined us unto the adoption of children by Jesus Christ to Himself, according to the good pleasure of His will.

To the praise of the glory of His grace, wherein He has made us accepted in the beloved. In whom we have redemption through His blood, the forgiveness of sins, according to the riches of His grace. Wherein He has abounded toward us in all wisdom and prudence. Having made known unto us the mystery of His will, according to His good pleasure which He has purposed in Himself; that in the dispensation of the fullness of time He might gather together in one all things in Christ, both which are in heaven and on earth, even in Him. In whom also we have obtained an inheritance, being predestined according to the purpose of Him who works all things after the counsel of His own will. That we should be to the praise of His glory, who first trusted in Christ, in whom ye also trusted, after that ye heard the Word of truth, the gospel of your salvation in whom also after that ye believed, ye were sealed with that Holy Spirit of promise, which is the earnest of our inheritance until the redemption of the possession, unto the praise of His glory.

May the God of our Lord Jesus Christ, the Father of glory, give unto you the spirit of wisdom and revelation in the knowledge of Him, the eyes of your understanding being enlightened that ye nay know what is the hope of His calling, and what the riches of the glory of His inheritance in the saints. And what is the exceeding greatness of His power toward us who believe, according to the working of His mighty power, which He wrought in Christ when He raised Him from the dead and set Him at His right hand in the heavenly places. Far above all principality and power, and might, and dominion, and every name that is named, not only in this world but also in that which is to come. And has put all things under His feet, and gave Him to be head over all things to the Church, which is His body, the fullness of Him that fills all in all," Ephesians 1:1-23.

Salvation-Confession of Sins

"If you confess with your mouth the Lord Jesus and believe in your heart that God raised Him from the dead, you shall be saved. For with the heart one believes unto righteousness and with the mouth confession is made unto salvation. For the Scripture says, 'Whoever be-lieves on Him will not be put to shame. For whoever calls upon the Name of the Lord shall be saved," Romans 10:9-1 3.

Jesus-Only Savior
"Let it be known to you all and to all the people of Israel that by the Name of Jesus Christ of Nazareth, whom you crucified, whom God raised from the dead, has become the chief cornerstone. And there is no salvation in any other name under heaven given to man by which we must be saved," Acts 4:10-12.

The Atonement
"God demonstrated His own love toward us that while we were yet still sinners, Christ died for us. much more then, having been jus-tified by His blood, we shall be saved from wrath through Him. For if when we were enemies, we were reconciled to God through the death of His Son, much more, having been reconciled, we shall be saved by His life," Romans 5:8-10.

Forgiveness of Sins
"In Him we have redemption through His blood, the forgiveness of sins, according to the riches of His grace," Ephesians 1:7.

Church-The Ground and Pillar of Truth
Hollywood, go to Church!
Church attendance is a must if one desires to attain salvation.

Apostle Paul wrote to Timothy, "I write so that you may know how to conduct yourself in the House of God, which is the House of the Living God, the pillar and ground of the truth," 1 Timothy 3:15.

The Church is the House of God where we learn about Him and where we grow and reach spiritual maturity. It is the place where one learns about Christ's path, which can lead to one's salvation. The Church is where divine things occur. It is a living body created by Christ.

Further, Scripture tells us, "Do not forsake the assembling of yourselves, as is the manner of some," Hebrews 10:24-25. This means not to abandon the Church. So we see here that we are commanded by God to attend Church.

North Korea Summit

President Trump has attended the North Korean Summit in which he succeeded in having North Korea sign the Denuclearization Document. President Trump at first cancelled this Summit, but at my urging, he reinstated it, and this was good. Hope all goes well from here on.

Meghan Markle Wedding

What an extravagant wedding it was! It was also very expensive! I don't remember Princess Diana's wedding to be this big and so extravagant. By the way, how expensive was Kate's wedding? Also, a big part of the forty-four-million of Meghan and Prince Harry's wedding went to pay for security, so I heard.

Wikipedia: Meghan Markle: Biography

Meghan, Duchess of Sussex, born Rachel Meghan Markle, August 1st, 1981, is an American born member of the British Royal Family and a former actress. Markle was raised in Los Angeles, California and has a mixed ethnic heritage. During her studies at Northwest University, she began playing small roles in television series and films. From 2011 to 2017, she played Rachel Zane on the American legal drama Suits. She is an outspoken feminist and has addressed issues of gender inequality and her lifestyle website, The Tig, featured a column profiling influential women. She represented international charity organizations and received recognition for her fashion and style, releasing a line of clothing in 2016.

Markle was married to actor and producer Trevor Engelson from 2011 until their divorce in 2013. In 2017 she announced her engagement to Prince Harry, grandson of Queen Elizabeth II, and she moved to London. She retired from acting, closed her related social media accounts, and started undertaking public engagements as part of the British royal family. She became Duchess of Sussex upon her marriage to Prince Harry in 2018. They have a son, Archie.

Rachel Meghan Markle was born in Los Angeles, California. Her mother, Doria Ragland, is a former social worker and yoga instructor, living with Meghan and Harry. Markle has often described having a very close friendship with her mother. Her father, Thomas Markle Sr., lives in Rosarito, Mexico and is a retired television director of photography and lighting director whose profession resulted in his young daughter often visiting the set of Married With Children. Markle's parents divorced when she was six-years-old. Her older paternal half siblings are Samantha Markle and Thomas Markle Jr.

Markle described her heritage in a 2015 essay of Elle, "My dad is Caucasian and my mom is African-American." Markle grew up in Hollywood. She was educated in private schools beginning at age two at the Hollywood Little Red Schoolhouse. Nick News with Linda Ellerbee profiled her successful campaign at age eleven to get Procter and Gamble to change a national television commercial that she viewed as sexist. She was raised as a Protestant, although she attended Immaculate Heart High School, an all-girl Catholic Private School in Los Angeles. She then attended Northwest University, where she joined Kappa Kappa Gamma sorority and participated in community service and charity projects. She also served an internship at the American Embassy in Buenos Aires and studied for one semester in Madrid, known in the United States as "junior year abroad." She received a Bachelor's Degree from Northwestern University School of Communication in 2003 with a double major in theater and international studies.

Illegal Immigration-Family Separations

President Trump's "Zero Tolerance Policy" on illegal immigration is separating families. Parents who migrate here illegally are put in jail and their children are taken away. This is disturbing and traumatic for both the parents and the children. I urged the President to find a way to keep families together. The following day, he promised not to separate families anymore. Many children have now been reunited with their families. I do not believe that arresting illegal parents is a solution. I believe that detaining parents and children together until their deportation is a better solution.

ICE

US Immigration and Customs Enforcement is a mission through the enforcement of more than 400 federal statues and focuses on smart immigration enforcement, preventing terrorism, and combatting the illegal movement of people and trade. Here is a letter I sent to President Trump concerning the protesters, including certain Hollywood stars who wanted to eliminate ICE because it is separating families.

"It seems like people jump to protest when they do not like a law such as ICE. They want it removed, so they can do whatever they want to do to fit their agenda. It's as if they want to do away with law and order. ICE helps to keep things in control. They enforce the law. But we should still try to keep families together. Maybe we need to review ICE and modify it."

I suggested for ICE to be reviewed to stop the separation of families. Trump has since stopped separating families and has united many children with their parents. Parents who migrate to US illegally with their children together are no longer being arrested and their children being put in protective custody. Parents and children are now being detained and held together until their court date and until they are deported back to their nation together.

Thai Cave Boys

The twelve Thai Cave Boys and their coach have finally been rescued from the cave after seventeen long days and nights. How tragic it was for them to have been in this dark cave so long and to starve for at least ten days. I thank God they are out. I wish them a speedy and whole recovery.

I invite the Thai Cave Boys to embrace Christianity for, "God so loved the world that He gave His one and only begotten Son, so that whosoever believes in Him will not perish but have everlasting life," John 3:16.

"Jesus is the propitiation for our sins, having given His life on the cross for the whole world," 1 John 2:2, and "There is none other name under heaven given among men whereby we must be saved,"Acts 4:12.

"All must turn to God in repentance and have faith in our Lord Jesus,"Acts 20:21.

Jesus said, "If you love Me, you will keep My Commandments," John 14:15.

Hollywood Suicides

Hollywood, as we all know, something tragic has happened to two stars. Let's keep in our prayers the families of Kate Spade and Anthony Bourdain who have committed suicide. Let's pray that their families be strengthened during these difficult times. Suicide is never easy on families who are left with the pain and suffering. Their loved ones are gone, and they feel an emptiness inside. For those who are contemplating suicide, there are to reach out to for help.

National Suicide Prevention Lifeline-1-800-273-8255

Suicide.com-Shares many problems which lead to suicide: Symptoms, Causes & Cures

Google:American Foundation for Suicide Prevention

Grief Scriptures

Hollywood, there are some grief Scriptures, no matter what the grief may be:

"Come to Me all who labor and are heavy laden and I will give you rest," Matthew 11:28.

"He heals the brokenhearted and binds up their wounds," Psalm 147:3.

"Humble yourselves under the mighty hand of God, that He may exalt you in due time, casting all your cares upon Him for He cares for you," 1 Peter 5:7.

"My flesh and my heart fail, but God is the strength of my heart and my portion forever," Psalm 73:26.

"Jesus wept," John 11:35.

Jesus weeps for us, cares about our trials, griefs, pains, and sufferings.

Suicide-Eternal Condemnation

There is eternal condemnation for those who take their own lives. They cannot be saved.

Scripture tells us that, "If you destroy the temple of God, God will destroy you for the temple of God is holy, which temple you are," 1 Corinthians 3:17.

Suicide Family Intervention

One who contemplates suicide can also reach out to family. Share with them your problems, your pains, and your thoughts of suicide. They can give good counsel and be of great comfort.

Scientology-Leah Remini

Leah Remini has exposed the falsehood of the Scientology Church and its abuses and has come out of Scientology. She is now coming against Catholicism, claiming it is false.

I agree that Catholicism is partially false and have written about its false teachings for many years. The Catholic religion embraces false and demonic teachings and traditions, which we will explore throughout this book. Catholics have taken out of and added to the Bible, but look at what the Holy Bible tells us about those who take out and add to the Bible, which is the Word of God

For I testify to anyone that hears the words of the prophecy of this book, "If any man shall add unto these things, God shall add unto him the plagues that are written in this book. And if any man shall take away from the words of the Book of this prophecy, God shall take away his part out of the Book of Life and out of the Holy City, and from the things which are written in this book. He which testifieth these things saith,'surely I come quickly. Amen. Even so, come quickly Lord Jesus," Revelation 22:18-20.

Catholicism: The Rosary

The Rosary is one addition to the Bible, and such practice by adherents to the Catholic religion leads to perdition. One does not need to pray repetitious prayers, such as Hail Mary, and beads are not necessary.

The Bible forbids repetitious prayers, "And when you pray, do not use vain repetitions as the heathens do. For they think that they will be heard for their many words," Matthew 6:7.

Prayer

"Hail Mary, Mother of God
Save us from the wrath to come."

We are not supposed to pray to Mother Mary. Scriptures tells us to pray to the Father and to the Father only.

"And whatever you ask the Father in My Name, He will give it to you," John 15:16 and John 16:23.

Selena Gomez-Medical Crisis

Selena Gomez, twenty-three, who suffers from lupus, had surgery to have a kidney transplant, which was donated to her by her fellow actress and best friend Francia Raisa. Thank God Selena made it, and thank God for her friend who was so gracious who also made it. God bless her for her heroic action. So how is the very beautiful Selena Gomez doing? A CNN source says she is doing just fine. She is healthy and is at home. And her friend is doing fine also. Now that's a very true friend Selena has!

Kid Rock for Michigan Senator?

No way! I told him to stay in music and play Christian lyrics. Music is a more suitable career for him.

Justin Bieber Engaged

Justin Bieber became engaged to Halley Baldwin. May they walk righteously before God and be blessed.

Me Too Movement

The Me Too Movement is an international movement against sexual harassment and sexual assault. Many female celebrities came forward claiming they are victims of sexual harassment and/or assault. In many cases, as it has been revealed to me through the Holy Spirit, I attribute this harassment and assault to provocative wear by many stars. Sexual harassment occurs also against men by women, although more rare, but it is rarely reported. However, men and women need to know that there are consequences for their actions. Stars, please treat each other well. Do not cross these boundaries, do not break trust in your friends. Be kind and compassionate toward one another. I observe the Me Too Movement victims of the movement and their assaults through visions and will bring them throughout the book, also with comments.

Larry Nasser Victims

May the Larry Nasser Victims get the support and relief they are searching for and may they heal from their traumas.

Demi Lovato Drug Overdose

Demi Lovato, twenty-five, has had an incident with drugs at her birthday party, which landed her in the hospital for about a week. She was found unconscious at her home and near fatally overdosed. She is now going to seek help at a drug rehab facility. This was a close call for Demi. Let's not forget about Bobbi Kristina Brown who overdosed on drugs in 2015 at age twenty-two, two years after her mother overdosed on drugs. They were both found dead in the bathtub. How tragic it is. All stars who have drug problems should seek help and do not let the drug gets out of control.

Jessica Vogel Fatal Drug Overdose

Hell's Kitchen Contestant Jessica Vogel, thirty-four, was not Demi Lovato. She died of a drug overdose on August 1st, 2018, seven days after Demi was found unconscious from a drug but survived. Jessica admitted she had a drug and alcohol problem, and in a video about her death, it was told that the damage the drugs did to her body was too great for her to survive. I am at a loss for words. It seems like this happens too often to too many dear people.

All stars who use drugs surrender to Christ for, "The Lord is not slack concerning His promises, as some count slackness, but is long-suffering toward us, not willing that any should perish, but that all should come to repentance," 2 Peter 3:9.

CALIFORNIA FIRES: 2018

News reports tell us there are:

600 homes destroyed

2,000 oyed

40,000 evacuees

90,000 acres burned

150 miles burned

9 people killed

Certain Hollywood Stars are in the path or not too far from the fires, and they should not wait until the last minute to evacuate as one person waited until the fire reached the back door of his home. This is very risky and dangerous. Fire spreads very quickly. If there are warnings of coming fires, stars should gather their most prized possessions and put them in storage and evacuate their homes.

Fortune Telling

Here's what the Bible tells us about fortune telling:

"You shall not practice divination or soothsaying," Leviticus 19:26b.

"I will cut off sorceries from your hand and you shall have no soothsayers," Micah 5:12.

Hollywood, do not practice fortune telling, go to fortune tellers or call fortune telling lines. It is sinful, and it grieves God. Fortune tellers work by the power of Satan and by guessing and manipulation. Same with magicians; they work through the power of Satan through hypnosis. It is very sinful. Do not practice magic and do not watch magicians. People who practice magic or watch magicians become demonically possessed.

Witchcraft, Soothsayers, Omens, Sorcerers, Mediums, Spiritists

"There shall not be found among you anyone who practices witchcraft, or a soothsayer, or one who interprets omens, or a sorcerer, or one who conjures spells (casts spells), or a medium, or a spiritist, or one who calls up the dead. For all who do these things are an abomination to the Lord," Deuteronomy 18:10-12.

"Give no regard to mediums or familiar spirits; do not seek after them, to be defiled by them," Leviticus 19:31.

"The person who turns to mediums or familiar spirits, I will set My face against that person," Leviticus 20:6.

Witchcraft is the practice and belief in magical skills and abilities.

Soothsayer is a person who is supposed to be able to foresee he future.

Omens is an even regarded as a portent of good or evil. People in ancient times believed that omens bring a divine message from their gods. These omens include natural phenomena, for example an eclipse, abnormal births of animals and humans and behavior of the sacrificial lamb on its way to the slaughter. They had specialist, the diviners, to interpret these omens. Another example: the dark clouds were considered a bad omen. Omens of things to come: Crows, in China and all Asian cultures, represent death, evil dark.

Sorcerer is a person who claims or is believed to have magic powers: a wizard, an occultist, a Diviner, a warlock, a voodooist, a witch, an enchanter, necromancer, magus. A necromancer communicates with the dead to foretell future events or discover hidden knowledge: to summon the spirit of the dead. A magus is a sorcerer.

Medium- is one who communicates with deceased loved ones and finds closure.

Spiritist-a spiritualistic philosophy and religion codified in the 19th century by Allen Karder. It proposed the study of the nature, origin and destiny of spirits and their relation with the corporal world.

The Bible forbids all these practices and beliefs.

Inspiration Quote

"I cannot give you the formula for success, but I can give you the formula for failure-try to please everybody."
Herbert Bayard Swope

Xenophobic. Xenophobic means, "prejudice against people from other countries." Let none be this way up in Hollywood.

Recipe: Meat Loaf

Three pounds of ground beef

Two eggs

Three slices of bread

Salt

Pepper

Garlic powder

Mix beaten eggs, bread, salt, pepper, and garlic powder. Shape into a rectangular loaf, top with barbecue sauce (sweet barbecue sauce is better) and bake in oven at 400 degrees for about twenty-five to thirty minutes. Serve with a side of mashed potatoes or a vegetable of your choice. Serves three to four. Good after Church lunch.

Did You Know?

Did you know that the Bible is made up of sixty-six books, thirty-nine books in the Old Testament, and twenty-seven books in the New Testament? And the Bible can be read in one year. Get a one year Bible reading calendar from your local Church or online: bibleinoneyear.org

Prophetic Word

"Call upon the Name of the Lord. He will never leave you nor forsake you. He will show you a new way and a new path. Your ways are not My ways. I am like an earthly Father and know you as My own. I created you and know all your needs. wants and desires says the Lord your God. Call upon Me for your family, to save your family cleanse you from all sins, to purify you, for I am a merciful God who sent My son to the cross for your redemption says the Lord."

Principles of Marriage
Premarital Sex-1 Corinthians 7:2-5

"It is good for a man not to touch a woman. Nevertheless, because of sexual immorality, let each man have his own wife, and let each woman have her own husband. Let the husband render to his wife the affection due her, and likewise also the wife to her husband. The wife does not have authority over her own body, but the husband does. And likewise the husband does not have authority over his own body, but the wife does. Do not deprive one another except with consent for a time, that you may give yourselves to fasting and prayer, and come together again so that Satan does not tempt you because of your lack of self-control."

Keep Your Marriage Vows-1 Corinthians 7:10-11

"Now to the married I, Paul, command, yet not I but the Lord: A wife is not to depart from her husband. But even if she does depart, let her remain unmarried or be reconciled to her husband. And a husband is not to divorce his wife."

Keep Your Bed Undefiled-Hebrews 13:4

"Marriage is honorable among all, and the bed undefiled, but fornicators and adulterers God will judge"

There is forgiveness for fornication and adultery. Here is God's promise of forgiveness, mercy, and redemption:

Our Compassionate High Priest-Hebrews 14-1 6.

"Seeing then that we have a Great High Priest has passed through the heavens, Jesus the Son of God, let us hold fast our profession. For we do not have a High Priest cannot sympathize with our weaknesses, but was in all things tempted as we are, yet without sin. Let us therefore come boldly before the throne of grace, that we may obtain mercy, and find grace to help in time of need."

Unbelieving Spouse-1 Corinthians 7:10-16

"But to the rest, I, not the Lord, say, If any brother has a wife who does not believe, and she is willing to live with him, let him not divorce her. And a wife who has a husband who does not believe, if he is willing to live with her, let her not divorce him. For the unbelieving husband is sanctified by the wife, and the unbelieving wife is sanctified by the husband: otherwise your children would be unclean, but now they are holy. But if the unbeliever departs, let him depart; a brother or a sister is not under bondage in such cases. But God has called us to peace. For, how do you know Oh wife whether you will save your husband? Or how do you know Oh husband whether you will save your wife?"

Be Ye Not Unequally Yoked: Christians Marrying Non-Christians-2 Corinthians 6:14-16.

"Do not be unequally yoked with unbelievers. For what fellowship has righteousness with lawlessness. And what communion has light with darkness? And what accord has Christ with Belial (Satan)? Or what part has a believer with an unbeliever? And what agreement has the temple of God with idols? For you are the temple of the living God, if Christ dwells in you."

These Scriptures mean that the Bible forbids Christians to marry non-Christians; or for Christians to have non-Christian friends. These relationships are forbidden by God. An unbeliever is a person who is not a Christian, not of Christian Faith. Concerning this matter, God further says:

"I will dwell in you, and walk among you.
I will be your God and you shall be My people."
Therefore,
Come out from among them
And be separate says the Lord.
Do not touch what is unclean,
And I will receive you.
I will be a Father to you
And you shall be My sons and daughters,
says the Lord Almighty," verses 17-18.

Some may say this book is divisive. Well, yes because not all receive the Gospel. But those who receive these Gospel messages can find redemption.

Entertainment: George Clooney

George Clooney is the highest paid actor from June 2017 to June 2018: $273 million

Aretha Franklin

The Queen of Soul, Aretha Franklin, passed away, August 18th, 2018. Thank you to all the stars who attended her funeral, who sang. Thank you to all Ministers, Pastors, government officials, and friends who came to our city of Detroit to pay your respects to our Queen of Soul Aretha Franklin. Her funeral was one of a kind. She will be remembered always.

> Quote: *"He who laughs, lasts."*
> Author Unknown

Me Too Movement

About the time Hollywood women come out, from actresses to politicians to anchorwomen, etc. This movement is long overdue, and I believe it will change the workforce, the social spectrum between men and women and even the laws.

Fatal Prescription Drug Overdose

We just had another drug overdose: Dennis Shields. A fatal mixture of drugs led to the fatal overdose of Real Housewives Bethenny Frankel's ex-partner Dennis Shields, fifty-one. He told police he took a combination of oxycodone, Vicodin, and a sleeping pill and alcohol. He had been prescribed numerous medications for a back injury.

Drugs: Effects

Cocaine

It is a powerfully addictive, psychoactive, stimulant drug. Cocaine's effect occurs in the midbrain region called the ventral tegmental area (VIA). Some users of cocaine report feelings of reusability and anxiety. Some deaths occur even with low doses.

Heroine

Heroin is an opioid most commonly used as a recreational drug for its euphoric effects. In certain countries, it is used to reduce pain.

Common Side Effects:

Respiratory depression

Dry mouth

Addiction

Meth

Meth is a stimulant drug usually used as a white, bitter-tasting powder or a pill. Crystal Methamphetamine is a form of the drug that looks like glass fragments or shiny bluish-white rocks. It is chemically similar to amphetamine (a drug used to treat attention deficit hyperactivity disorder-ADHD, and narcolepsy, a sleep disorder). Other common names for Methamphetamine are: chalk, crank, crystal, ice, meth and speed.

Long Term Effects:

Extreme weight loss

Severe dental problems

Intense itching leading to skin sores from scratching

Anxiety

Confusion

Sleeping problems

Violent Behavior

Paranoia, extreme and unreasonable distrust of others

Hallucinations, sensations and images that seem real though they aren't

In addition prolonged use of methamphetamine causes changes in the brain's dopamine system that are associated with reduced co-ordination and impaired verbal learning. Over the long-term, changes also affect areas of the brain involved with emotion and memory, even an increased risk of developing Parkinson's disease, a disorder of the nerves that affect movement.

Fentanyl

Fentanyl is used to produce anesthesia for surgery to treat pain before, during, and after surgery. This drug is said to be one of the most lethal drugs, much more powerful than cocaine. Even a small amount can kill a person.

Pregnant/Nursing Women: Marijuana
Marijuana

The legalization of marijuana has opened the door for pregnant/nursing mothers to embrace this drug. They justify it by say-ing it is legalized now. Just because it is legalized now does not mean it is not dangerous and harmful for mom and baby. Cigarettes are le-galized also, yet they kill 480,000 people annually, including deaths from second-hand smoke.

Alcohol

It is dangerous and harmful for mom and baby also. There are 88,000 alcohol-related deaths in the US annually. World-wide alcohol re-lated deaths stand at 2.5 million annually. Staggering high number, huh?

First Commandment of Christ:

"You shall love the Lord your God with all your heart, with all your soul and with all your mind," Matthew 22:37.

Second Commandment of Christ:

"You shall love your neighbor as yourself," Matthew 22:39.

Do Not Turn Evil for Evil

"See that no one renders evil for evil to anyone, but always pursue what is good both for yourselves and for all," 1 Thessalonians 5:15.

Daily News

Dolores O 'Riordan: Alcohol Bathtub Drowning

Singer Dolores O'Riordan, forty-six, died in her hotel bathtub after a night of drinking. Police ruled her death an accidental drowning. She had an alcohol blood level more than four times the legal limit in Britain when she died January 15th, 2018. She was submerged, clothed, and face up in the tub. Her death is drawing attention to the dangers of boozing and bathing. Coroners also cited atherosclerotic heart disease and cocaine as contributing factors.

I am wondering why Dolores would get in the tub to bathe fully clothed, unless she was killed, drowned by somebody, or unless she was so drunk that she forgot to undress. Something is not right in this case.

Eating Disorders

Wikipedia: Anorexia

Anorexia is an eating disorder characterized by low weight, fear of gaining weight, and a strong desire to be thin, resulting in food restrictions. Many people with anorexia see themselves as being overweight, even though they are underweight. If asked they usually deny they have a problem with low weight. Often they weigh themselves frequently, eat only small amounts, and only eat certain foods. Some will exercise excessively, force themselves to vomit, or use laxatives to produce weight loss. Complications may include osteoporosis, infertility, and heart damage among others. Women will often stop having menstrual periods. I have observed such behaviors in Hollywood. Stars need to eat right, eat until full, especially if pregnant or nursing.

Wikipedia: Bulimia

Bulimia is an eating disorder characterized by binge eating followed by purging. Binge eating means eating a large amount of food in a short amount of time. Purging means to get rid of the food consumed. This may be done by vomiting or laxatives. Other efforts to lose weight may include the use of diuretics, stimulants, water fasting, or excessive exercise. Most people with bulimia are at normal weight. The forcing of vomiting may result in thickened skin on the knuckles and breakdown of the teeth. Bulimia is usually associated with other mental disorders, such as depression, anxiety, and problems with drugs and alcohol. There is also a higher risk of suicide or self-harm.

Wikipedia: Obesity

Obesity is a medical condition in which excess body fat to the extent that it may have a negative effect on health. People are generally considered obese when their body mass index (BMI), a measurement obtained by dividing a person's weight by the square of the person's height, is over 30kg/rn2, with the range 25-30kg/m2, defined as overweight.

Obesity increases the likelihood of various diseases and conditions, particularly cardiovascular diseases, type two diabetes, obstruction sleep apnea, certain types of cancers, osteoarthritis, and depression.

Obesity is most commonly caused by a combination of excessive food intake, lack of physical activity, and genetic susceptibility. A few cases are caused primarily by genes, endocrine disorders, medical or mental disorders. The view that obese people eat little yet gain weight due to a slow metabolism is not medically supported. On average obese people have a greater energy expenditure than their normal counterparts due to the energy required to maintain an increased body mass.

Obesity is mostly preventable through a combination of social changes and personal choices. Changes to diets and exercising are the main treatments. Diet quality can be improved by reducing the consumption of energy-dense foods, such as those high in fats or sugars and by increasing the intake of dietary fiber (fruits, vegetables, grains). Medications can be used to help with weight loss; check with your doctor first. Gastric bypass surgery can help also.

Obesity is a leading preventable cause of death world-wide with increasing rates in adults and children. In 2015, 600 million adults (12%) and 100 million children were obese in 195 countries. Obesity is more common in women than men. The American Medical Association classified obesity as a disease.

Writing this book is somewhat challenging due to my medical situation. I have colon and stomach cancer and cancer in other organs also. It is difficult to sit and write due to a large tumor in the abdomen. Many times I write by lying halfway down. I have to type with one hand at a time because my hands tire. My right hand is half way clenched many times due to diabetes. I have suffered with this cancer for over eleven years.

Fulfilling The Law of Christ

"Bear one another's burdens, and so fulfill the Law of Christ." – Galatians 6:2

What does it mean to bear each other's burdens?

A good example is the Selena Gomez Case. Her friend Raisa stepped in and saved her life with a kidney transplant. Arias took this burden upon herself, a very humble thing to do. We may not all be called to take on such big burdens or to make such big sacrifices, but we are all called to help people in time of need. Have a friend who just had a baby? Offer to babysit a day, so parents can catch up on some sleep. Know someone close who's ill? Offer help with housekeeping, cooking once or twice a week or maybe more, help even with grocery shopping. And so on. Your good deeds will not remain hidden. You will be rewarded by Our God the Father.

Me Too Movement

Had a meeting at a hotel with four men from my Church and was disgraced by them. Wish I had not gone.

Slander

"Whoever secretly slanders his neighbor, him I will destroy," Psalm 101:5a.

Slander-Dictionary– "the action or crime of making false spoken statements damaging to a person's reputation."

Slander is maligning one's character, vicious verbal attacks, things not true which brings a person shame, degradation and defamation of character. God hates it when you slander your neighbor. Your neighbor can be your brother, sister, co-worker, your friend, your fellow star, your boss, your President, your lawmaker, your spouse, your enemy, and so on. But here is a prayer for forgiveness:

"Be merciful to me O Lord,
For I cry to you all day long.
Rejoice the soul of your servant.
For to You, o Lord, I lift up my soul.
For You Lord, are good,
And ready to forgive,
And abundant in mercy to all
Those who call upon you."
Psalm 86:3-5

God's Grace
You, O Lord, are a God
full of compassion, and
gracious,
Longsuffering and abundant in
mercy and truth."
Psalm 86:15

Bible Names
The Bible has a few names:
The Holy Bible
Holy Scriptures
The Word
The Sword

Wikipedia: Transcendental Meditation

Transcendental Meditation refers to a specific form of silent meditation. Maharishi Mahesh Yogi introduced the TM technique and TM movement in India in the mid-1950's. TM became more popular in the 1960s and 1970s, and his meditation technique was practiced by celebrities. The TM Organization has grown to include educational programs, health products, and related services.

The TM technique involves the use of a sound called a mantra and is practiced for fifteen to twenty minutes twice daily. The TM movement is a non-religious method for relaxation, stress reduction, and self development. The technique has been seen as both religious and non-religious. The United States Court of Appeals upheld the federal ruling that TM was essentially "religious in nature" and therefore could not be taught in public schools.

Transcendental Meditation involves the use of a mantra for fifteen to twenty minutes twice daily while sitting with the eyes closed. TM has been described as an aspect of a new religious movement, as rooted in Hinduism, and as a non-religious practice for self-development.

What is a mantra? A mantra is a sacred utterance, a numinous sound, a syllable, word or phonemes, or group of words in Sanskirt believed by practitioners to have psychological and spiritual powers. Mantra meditation helps to induce an altered state of consciousness. A mantra may or may not have a syntactic structure or literal meaning. It also contains hymns, chants, compositions.

I bring news that Transcendental Meditation is demonic meditation because it has its roots in Hinduism. Hinduism is one of the leading false world religions with demonic rituals, beliefs, and practices.

Hollywood, meditate on the Bible. It is the best meditation. Meditate on the Psalms and Proverbs. And you can also meditate on your life without incorporating any meditations of false religions. To meditate means to "think," to "dwell" on something, to "give deep thought to."

Bible Meditation

Bible Meditation is best, "This book of the Law shall not depart from thy mouth, but thou shall meditate therein day and night, that thou may observe to do according to all that is written therein; for then thou shall make thy way prosperous, and then thou shall have good success," Joshua I :8.

Why Is Hinduism a False /Demonic Religion?

First, Hinduism, an Indian religion, is a false religion because it does not sustain belief or teachings of the Deity of God and His Son Jesus Christ. Second, Hinduism has many false and demonic teachings, beliefs, and practices. "Having demonic teachings" means that the teachings are "the teachings of demons: teachings and beliefs dictated by demons in people's heads." The Hindus also have many idols (statues), which they worship, another practice/ritual forbidden by God. Hollywood, steer clear of Hinduism and its practices.

Hindu Deity

Hinduism, a Polytheistic faith (belief in many gods) has many Deities, but here are the dominant ones: Shiva, Brahma, Vishnu, Shaktism.

Yoga

It is the same scenario with yoga as is with Transcendental Meditation. Yoga derives from Hinduism, it has demonic roots, and should not be practiced, even if no chanting or singing occurs. Yoga meditation is very popular in Hollywood. If one wants to argue on this matter, do your own research online and also seek more Pastoral help. We can do regular exercise without calling it yoga.

Karate and Tae Kwan Dow are achieved through demonic powers. Steer clear of these sports.

Buddhists, turn to Jesus Christ, Buddhism is not the way neither.

"Repent ye therefore and be converted, that your sins may be blotted out, when the times of refreshing shall come upon you from the Lord," Acts 3:19.

LGBTQ's

For those who want salvation, come out of your sexual lifestyle. If you were married and are now divorced, you must reconcile with your former spouse, if possible.

Many believe that God made them gay and this is not true. Romans 1 calls homosexuality and lesbianism an abomination. God is holy and does not make anyone gay, so they can sin. He is too holy for that. God says to turn from your ways. Here are Scriptures:

"Repent then, and turn to God, so that your sins may be blotted out, that times of refreshing may come upon you from the Lord," Acts 3:19.

"For the Lord your God is gracious and compassionate. He will not turn His face from you if you return to Him," 2 Chronicles 30:9b.

"I tell you no! But unless you repent, you will all likewise perish," Luke 13:3.

Repentance Prayer-The Sinner's Prayer
Dear God
I know I'm a sinner and I ask for
your forgiveness.

I believe Jesus Christ is your Son I believe that He died
for my sin and that you raised
Him to life.
I want to trust Him as my Savior
and follow Him as Lord
from this day forward.

Guide my life and help me to
do Your will. I pray this in the
Name of Jesus.
Amen

After this prayer, you can start attending a Church and ask them for a Bible also.

Body Tattooing

Body tattooing is sin. Leave your body as God made it. Tattooing your body is also a cancer risk because tattooing ink carries carcinogen, a cancer causing chemical.

Stand Your Ground Law

This is a law that authorizes a person to protect and defend one's own life and limb against threat or perceived threat. Everyone, be cautious in this matter.

Black Lives Matter

Black Lives Matter is an internationally activist movement originating in the African-American community that campaigns against violence, systematic racism toward black people. Black Lives Matter regularly hold protests speaking out against police killings of black people and broader issues such as racial profiling, police brutality, and racial inequality in the United States Criminal Justice System.

Quote: *"People who hurt you teach you the greatest lessons in life."*
Author Unknown

Romanian Potato Salad

Peel five potatoes, cut in two-inch triangles, and boil until tender. Drain water. Add oil, vinegar, salt, and onion, cut lengthwise. Done.

Hollywood, Steer Clear of Eating Blood!

"Apostle James said, 'I judge that we should not judge those from among the Gentiles who are turning to God, but that we should write to them to abstain from things polluted by idols, from sexual immorality, from things strangled and from blood," Acts 15:20-22. Here's the meaning:

To abstain from things polluted by idols means: not to eat food made for idols, or practice pagan rituals and ceremonies.

Wikipedia: "In days of old, the leaders of different communities would make for themselves statues of creatures, then to obtain obedience from the general population, they would say that the creature (statue), would kill or devour them if they did not work as expected. To continue with the illusion, feasts were assembled and pagan priests would do what they could to make it appear that the statue was eating. Or sacrifices were made to make the illusion appear that the statue killed someone."

Statues are called idols. Do not eat things offered to idols. Hindus feed some of their statues. Do not eat that food. Do not even be in their temples to see their statues. Evil dwells in these temples.

To abstain from sexual immorality means: abstain from sex out of wedlock and to the married, abstain from committing adultery.

To abstain from things strangled means: do not eat strangled animals. For example do not eat a chicken which was strangled. It suffered enough in the killing.

To abstain from blood means do not eat meat with blood still in it. For example if your steak is still bleeding on your plate, throw it back in the pan! No more medium/rare steaks. Try medium to well-done. Your steak can be pinkish as long as it's not bleeding.

Why is it sin to eat meat with blood?

"For the life of the flesh, the animal, is in the blood," Leviticus 17:11. This was a Mosaic Law in the Old Testament. Let's see what it says.

"Whatever man of the house of Israel, or of the strangers who dwell among you, who eats any blood, I will set My face against that person and will cut him off from among his people. For the life of the flesh is in the blood and I have given it to you at the altar to make atonement for your souls," Leviticus 1 7:10-1 1.

We no longer need the blood of animals to make atonement for our sins. Now Jesus is our propitiation. His blood makes atonement for our sins. So you say that we no longer need the animal's blood for our sins, however, this law also stands in the New Testament. Does not common sense tell you not to eat animal blood?

You may say that God sanctified the animal in the New Testament and nothing is unclean, therefore you can eat rare meat. Not so! Yes, God sanctified all things, but in Acts 15:20, which is in the New Testament, we are commanded not to eat blood.

You may say the command not to eat blood does not refer to meat but to something else. Well, Acts 15:20 refers us to Old Testament Scriptures, where God left an everlasting ordinance which tells about eating blood from meat. Let's go there:

1. "This shall be a perpetual statute throughout your generations in all your dwellings: you shall eat neither fat nor blood," Leviticus 3:17.

2. "But you shall not eat flesh (meat) with its life, that is its blood," Genesis 9:4.

3. "Only you shall not eat the blood; you shall pour it on the earth like water," Deuteronomy 12:16.

4. "Only be sure that you do not eat the blood; for the blood is the life; you may not eat the life with the meat," Deuteronomy 12:23.

    You would not take your plate with steak on it, pour the blood in a cup, and drink it, would you? Well, it's the same thing if you eat it off the plate.

Here's what you can make tonight:
Sweet Barbecue Ribs and Potatoes

Season your ribs, you know the drill: rub them with oil, add salt, garlic, pepper (optional). Bake at 400 degrees for about forty minutes, until tender; when tender, add sweet barbecue sauce on both sides until done. Potatoes should be put in the same pan with ribs when the ribs are put in, and they should be done at the same time ribs are done. Cut potatoes in half lengthwise and season with salt. Serve.

Mac Miller: Rapper-Producer- Dead at 26-CNN

Mac Miller has been open in the past about his battles with substance addiction. He talked openly about his sobriety in a 2016 Vogue Profile saying he's changing how he lives life, getting sober, and his state of mind.

I have to admit this about myself. I, too, tried a drug, a Hawaiian joint when I was sixteen in high school. A friend in my swimming class offered it to me. We were swimming partners, teaching one another to swim. I had a near death experience from it, and I never touched drugs again. I told him about my experience, and he said it may have been laced with something. However, I have been a cigarette smoker off and on all throughout my life and I rarely ever touch alcohol, usually wine. I am not proud of myself. My best advice is to never start smoking, never try any drug. It can kill you the first time. Just say no.

Burt Reynolds
My condolences to Burt Reynold's Family. 09-2018

Entertainment: Hollywood Highest Paid Actress

Emma Stone is currently Hollywood's highest paid actress, making twenty-six-million for her Oscar winning performance in La La Land.

Forbes
Best Hollywood Movies of 2018-ETIMES

Searching	The Incredibles 2
Deadpool 2	You Were Never Really Here
Avengers: Infinity War	A Quiet Place
Alphaq	Ready Player One
Mission: Impossible–Fallout	Lady Bird

Ant Man and the Wasp	Three Billboards Outside Ebbing, Missouri
Isle of Dog	The Shape of Water
Hereditary	Black Panther
Phantom Thread	Darkest Hour
Paddington 2	The Post

The Best Movies of All Times

The Godfather	The Shawshank Redemption
Pulp Fiction	Star Wars
The Dark Knight	Jurassic Park
Goodfellas	Indiana Jones and the Raiders of the Lost Ark
The Godfather Part II	Gladiator
Schindler's List	The Lord of the Rings
The Matrix	Braveheart
Apocalypse Now	Titanic

The list is longer, but these are the major ones. Many of these movies are not fitting for Christians. We need more family-oriented movies, PG-13, non-violent and no sexual or profane content.

Harry Potter Movie

The Harry Potter movie has been an obsession upon this nation, teaching young children about witchcraft, wizards, magic, and so on. Demonic possessions occur in children who deal with witchcraft and magic and casting spells. All these children will perish and their parents who allow these things in their homes. Turn to God and ask for forgiveness and salvation, and the producer needs to do the same and also apologize to the United States for infesting this nation with witchcraft. Only God, the merciful one, can cleanse of all sins. Throw out the Harry Potter movies, books, toys, and so forth.

Pokémon

The same goes for Pokémon, where children have learned many evils, including casting spells. Hollywood, do not allow your children to watch Pokémon. Throw out all Pokémon toys, books, etc. Parents are responsible for what enters their home, and they are accountable to God for their children for what they see, hear, learn, and practice.

ER Actress Vanessa Marquez Dead

ER Actress Vanessa Marquez, forty-nine, was killed by California Police after she armed herself with a weapon that turned out to be a BB gun.

I believe Marquez wanted to go out this way. This is the reason she pointed the BB gun at police. She knew doing so would prompt police to shoot her. It is sad. She was distraught while police were trying to reason with her.

Is It Sin To:

Drive and text? Drink and drive?

Blow a red light?

Blow a stop sign?

Go above speed limit?

Ignore no U turn signs?

To illegally pass someone?

To run from the scene of an accident?

Yes, anytime you break the law, you sin, for it is written, "Let every soul be subject to the governing authorities. For there is no authority except from God, and authorities that exist are appointed by God," Romans 13:1.

So we see that those who make the laws, including traffic laws, are governing authorities appointed by God.

Is it sin to flick the finger at someone on the road or anywhere?

Yes, all the more. Not all stars do this but many do.

Road Rage

And shouting names and obscenities at someone in road rage is sin, too. Try to remain calm in stressful commuting situations.

Is It Sin To:

Steal from the department store?

Yes, "Let him who stole steal no longer, but rather let him labor, working with his hands what is good, that he may have something to give to him who has need," Ephesians 4:28.

For the few who do this, please pay for your merchandise, no matter how small, you can afford to pay it.

Is It Sin To:

Not help someone in need?

Yes, "To him who knows to do good but does not do it, to him it is sin," James 4:17.

Be Imitators of God

"Be ye imitators of God, as dear children, and walk in love as Christ also has loved us, and has given Himself for us an offering and a sacrifice to God for a sweet-smelling aroma. But fornication and all uncleanness, or covetousness, let it not be mentioned among you, as becometh saints. Neither filthiness nor foolish talking, nor jesting, which are not convenient, but rather giving of thanks. For this ye know that no whoremonger, nor unclean person, nor covetous man who is an idolater has any inheritance in the Kingdom of Christ and of God. Let no man deceive you with vain words, for because of these things comes the wrath of God upon the children of disobedience. Be not ye therefore partakers with them. For ye were sometimes darkness, but now you are light in the Lord; walk as children of light. For the fruit of the Spirit is in all goodness, righteousness and truth," Ephesians 5:1-9.

What is Fornication?

Fornication is sex out of wedlock which is sin. Repent. Repent means to stop.

Put on The New Man

"And that ye put on the new man which after God is created in righteousness and true holiness. Wherefore putting away lying, speak every man truth with his neighbor, for we are members one of another. Be angry but do not sin. Do not let the sun go down on your anger. Neither give place to the devil. Let him that stole steal no more, but rather let him labor, working with his hands the thing which is good, that he may have to give to him that needeth. Let no corrupt communication proceed out of your mouth, but that which is good to the use of edifying, that it may minister grace to the hearers. And grieve not the Holy Spirit of God, whereby ye are sealed unto the day of redemption. Let all bitterness, wrath, anger and clamour and evil speaking be put away from you, with all malice. And be ye kind one to another, tenderhearted, forgiving one another, even as God for Christ's sake has forgiven you," Ephesians 4:24-32.

The Body of Christ

The Body of Christ is the Church, "For as we have many members in one body, and all members have not all the same office. So we, being many, are one body in Christ, and everyone members one of another," Romans 12:4-5.

Christ-The Head of the Church

"Christ is the Head of the Church, He, Himself being the Savior of the body," Ephesians 5:23.

Hate Speech

Hate speech is a speech that attacks a person or group on the basis of attributes such as race, religion, ethnic origin, national origin, sex, disability, sexual orientation, or gender.

I am addressing an issue which we mostly associate hate speech with and this is homosexuality/lesbianism. Preachers speak against homosexuality and lesbianism because we are called to call out sin and to help people come out of sin. We love people and are merciful on them and do not want them to perish. We want all to be saved. We do not consider peaching against these sins to be "hate speech." We are called to preach the Word of God.

Facebook Post

Here is a post I recently ran across on Facebook titled: "Our Culture Has Accepted Two Huge Lies."

The first is that "If you disagree with someone's lifestyle, you must fear or hate them." Luminita: I agree. This is where the terms such as homophobic and Islamaphobic come from.

The second is that, "To love someone means you agree with everything they believe and do. Both are nonsense. You don't have to compromise convictions to be compassionate." Luminita: I agree with this, too.

Homosexuality and lesbianism are sins according to the Book of Romans, "Women exchanged the natural use for what is against nature. Likewise, also the men, leaving the natural use of the woman, burned in their lust for one another, men with men committing what is shameful, and receiving in themselves the penalty of their error which was due," Romans 1:26-27.

God Hates Divorce!

"For the Lord God of Israel says that He hates divorce. For it covers one's garment with violence. Therefore, take heed to your spirit, that you do not deal treacherously," Malachi 2:16. And, "What God has joined together, let no man separate," Matthew 19:6.

Let's find out about me now. Who am I?

I am the Spiritual Mother of this Nation and Mother of Hollywood. I am called to preach the Gospel to this nation and to win many souls to Christ. God is fulfilling the number of the Gentiles who must be saved through me, be it that I am the Mother of the Bride also. Mother of the Bride means being the Spiritual Mother of Christ's Church: the mother of all the people on earth who get saved, and this also makes me the Spiritual Mother of the earth. I am called to evangelize globally and to save people globally.

I was born in Bucharest, Romania in 1970 but was raised in the United States since age nine. I am divorced with six children. I am a beef, steak, and potato gal, in case I move to Hollywood and you invite me in your home, with tiramisu or any other for dessert. I love shrimp dishes, too, but please no muscles, whole lobster, clams, oysters, crab, crawfish, or octopus for me!

Me Too Movement Poem

> So we're meeting at a hotel
> I walk in and see the bed
> An amenity enticing for a rape
> Alone in a hotel I should not have met this man
> Now I have to always carry my shame
> For business I should have invited him in my home
> Where with him I am not alone
> Where I am surrounded by those I love
> Men and women should never meet alone
> But I fell in his trap
> Now I feel like a disgraced tramp

Me Too Movement

Why meet at a hotel? Why not meet at a restaurant or rent a convention room at the public library. Some rooms can accommodate twelve individuals or more.

> Quote:
> *For fast acting relief, try slowing down."*
> Lily Tomlin

Youth: Ten Questions to Ask On A First Date by Beliefnet

The first answer to the question is by Beliefnet. The second answer is by me marked by my name.

1. What is your favorite thing to do in your spare time?
    This question can somewhat tell you who a person is.
    Luminita: It also tells you if your hobbies, likes, dislikes are compatible.

2. What is your favorite movie/song? Gives you insight into who they are.
    Luminita: This tells you if you are compatible, if you like the same movies/music. You don't want to pear up with someone who does not like the music you like, or one who loves horror movies, which you hate or which frighten you.

3. Who are the most important people in your life?
    This gives insight into their world.
    Luminita: If he says his mother is one of the most important, you might have a good catch! Also, who are his friends?
    There's a saying, "Tell me who your friends are and I will tell you who you are." A person's friends are very influential in one's life.

4. What makes you laugh? Cry?
    This question also gives you insight into people's hearts/minds.
    Luminita: Are they soft hearted, merciful? Or are they non-chalant about almost anything.

5. If you could meet anyone in the world right now, who would it be and why?
    This tells us what is important to them.
    Luminita: Example, if the answer is the President, then we can say this person likes politics and cares about the issues around us. If this person wants to meet a singer or actress, this person is into music and likes entertaining. Hope no one wishes to meet a fictional movie character, then this person would be silly and not too serious-takes life lightly, or they just have a sense of humor above average. This person can be fun, too!

6. What is your favorite book of the Bible?
   This question shows their knowledge of the Bible.
   Luminita: Are you compatible here? Do you both have mutual respect for the Bible? Do you both attend Church? This area is very important to be compatible in. If you are a religious person and go to Church and the other person is not, then you have a problem. You don't want to marry someone who is not religious and will not accompany you to Church, or he is somewhat religious but not as serious as you. It will be a point of conflict your whole life, in just about every issue of life, even in the most important part of family life, which is child rearing. Be careful!

7. What's your favorite Bible verse. Shows what is of interest to him. Gives you insights.

8. If you could travel, where would you go?
   This shows if you have matching travel goals.

9. Where do you see yourself five years from now
   Gives you insight into their future.
   Luminita: It tells you of their dreams, tells you if you are compatible in goals. It also helps you both to maybe compromise on plans, change things, or come up with goals you both totally agree with.

10. What is your most memorable experience with God?
    This tells you how deep his/her relationship is with God. Are you compatible in this area?

I have a few questions of my own:
1. Are you accepted by his/her family? Make sure the answer is yes. You want to have nice in-laws, have a good relationship with them. Make sure you're accepted by the rest of his/her family, even close friends.

2. Do you both agree on child-rearing issues. Do you both agree to corporal punishment or does one use other disciplinary techniques?

3. Are you compatible in the hygiene department? Does person need a little improvement? Are they willing to make the improvement, or do they not give that much importance to their appearance? Avoid such dates.
4. Can your date cook? Do you both like to cook together?
5. Is your date a neat, orderly person or kinda messy? Being incompatible in this area can be of very high conflict, even leading to divorce. Make sure you are alike here.

Here's a helpful quote: "Life is too complicated not to be orderly."
Martha Stewart

Since we're on the subject of Martha Stewart, Let's see one of her recipes:

Instant Pot Chicken Curry

Ingredients
  One quarter cup ghee or vegetable oil
  One yellow onion thinly sliced (two cups)
  Kosher salt and freshly ground black pepper
  One tablespoon grated fresh ginger
      (from a two-inch peeled piece)
  One tablespoon grated garlic (from four cloves)
  Two tablespoons tomato paste
  Two teaspoon cumin seeds, lightly crushed
  Two teaspoons coriander seeds, lightly crushed
  One teaspoon Spanish paprika
  One cinnamon stick
  Three quarter cup low-sodium chicken broth or water
  Two pounds boneless skinless chicken thighs cut into
      one-inch pieces
  Steamed rice, warmed flatbread, yogurt, fresh cilantro leaves,
and lime wedges

Step 1

Melt ghee in a six-quart multicooker set to the high "sauté" setting. Add onion and season with salt and pepper. Cook, stirring often, until soft and golden brown, ten to twelve minutes. Add ginger, garlic, tomato paste cumin, coriander, paprika, chili powder, and cinnamon stick, cook, stirring until fragrant, one to two minutes, stir in broth.

Step Two

Toss chicken with one teaspoon salt and one quarter teaspoon black pepper, add to pot. Secure lid of multicooker, adjust vent to seal. Cook on high "Pressure Cook" setting for four minutes. Once time is complete, turn off machine and manually release pressure, carefully remove lid. Serve curry over steamed rice with warmed flatbread, yogurt, cilantro leaves, and lime wedges on the side.

Now back to the article by Beliefnet.

The following two questions may be the most important, determining whether a marriage will survive and be successful or fail.

Dual-Religion Marriages

6. Are you of the same religion?

Imagine you are Christian dating a Muslim. You wish to go to Church, your possible spouse goes to a Mosque. You believe in Jesus, he does not. Will you two worship separately, him at the Mosque and you at Church? How do you feel knowing your spouse will not attend Church with you? Who gets to see the children at holidays: the Christian family or the Muslim family? Would you and the children celebrate holidays, Easter, Thanksgiving, Christmas at Church, while your husband stays home be it that he doesn't celebrate Christmas, Easter due to his unbelief in Jesus? Or would he accompany you? Will the children be raised Christian or Muslim? Dual religions in a marriage can be a major area of conflict, even tearing a marriage apart. Many marriages in the United States are

like this: tumultuous and unhappy, many times even dangerous. Children are many times made to pick between the parents. And last in a dual religion marriage, each one of you
would continuously try to convert the other. This is no way
to live. Please be compatible in religion.

Dual-Cultural Marriages

7. Are you of the same race?
    Couples with different racial backgrounds may encounter
    certain problems including alienation, exclusion, and racism.

    Quote:"
    *If you wish to travel, travel light, take off all your
    envies, jealousies, unforgiveness, selfishness and fear."*
    Author-Glenn Clark

Me Too Movement

Feel uncomfortable about meeting with a male concerning business? Take along your father or any male in your life, a brother, uncle,
neighbor, or any close male friend.

Is it Sin To:

Buy a nice dress, wear it, and return to the department store and
cause a scandal because you are denied a refund? Yes, it is sin. Ladies,
stop fussing. Some of you even put the tags on and say you did not
wear it. You also rant and rage about high prices on merchandise, saying you can get it cheaper out of Hollywood territory. Then do so!

Is it sin to dye hair, have cosmetic surgery, breast implants, have
sex change?

Yes, it is sin. Leave yourself as God made you.

Bible Quiz

1. The trial of your faith works_____

   great works

   out our salvation

   patience

   righteousness

   Answer: James 1:3

2. God resists the _____ and gives the humble

   rich

   low-esteemed

   educated

   proud

   Answer: 1 Peter 5:5

3. Who is the first man recorded in the Bible as living in a cave?

   Adam

   Enoch

   Lot

   Cain

   Answer: Genesis 19:30

4. Where envy and strife is _____

   there also lurks envy and murder

   there is no rest

   there is confusion and every evil work

   there is famine and distress

   Answer: James 3:16

5. Did Jesus drink wine?

   He only transformed water into wine

   yes

   it's not mentioned

   only until He was 30

   Answer: Luke 7:34

Wikipedia: Strife

Anger or bitter disagreement, conflict. Scripture warns us about strife, "If you bite and devour one another, beware lest you be consumed (eaten up, destroyed) by one another," Galatians 5:15.

Wikipedia: Friendship

A relationship of mutual affection between two or more people. It is a stronger form of interpersonal bond than an association. Scripture tells us that "Greater love has no one than this, that he lay down his life for his friends," John 15:13, and our friends can shape us into who we are, "As iron sharpens iron, so a friend sharpens a friend, "Proverb 27:17. But friends can also min us, "Do not be deceived, bad company corrupts good character, "I Corinthians 15:33. Friendship is so important that the Word cautions us against having too many, "A man of many friends comes to ruin, "Proverb 18:24a, but "There is a friend who sticks closer than a brother," Proverb 18:24b. So Hollywood, be careful who your friends are. Choose them carefully. A reckless person is not a good choice for a friend because he will make you reckless also. Remember, bad company corrupts good character. An alcoholic or someone brawler or a gossiper or someone who is continuously in trouble with the law is not a good choice for a friend. Be wise, Hollywood!

Love Your Enemies

"You have heard that it was said, 'u shall love your neighbor and hate your enemy.' But I say to you, 'Love your enemies, bless those who curse you, do good to those who hate you, and pray for those who spitefully use you and persecute you, that you may be sons of your Father in heaven; for He makes His sun rise on the evil and on the good, and sends rain on the just and on the unjust," Matthew 5:43-45

Melania: Be Best-Bullying

Melania-Be Best, a children's agenda with a focus on social media. Her endeavor to stop school bullying may be a long road, but I believe she can curtail it.

Quote:
"I have learned to seek my happiness by limiting my desires, rather than attempting to satisfy them."
Author Stuart Mil

Hollywood, Bathe Your Children Daily

"Let us draw near with a pure heart in full assurance of faith, having our hearts sprinkled from an evil conscience, and our bodies washed with pure water," Hebrews 10:22.

Not all stars bathe their children daily; and your teenage children should practice these daily washing habits also.

Me Too Movement

Women unintentionally provoke their rape by meting alone with a man. Not all men are disciplined when they are alone with a woman.

Me Too Movement

Women unintentionally put themselves at risk of assault or harassment by men by wearing provocative clothing.

Nine Phrases That Signify Zero Respect in A Relationship by Beliefnet
1. I don't care.
   This is counterintuitive
2. Why does that matter to you?
   This signifies their feelings are not valid or relevant. It does not allow partner to have feelings, varying opinions, or beliefs.
3. That shouldn't bother you.
   This is a classic shutdown phrase of a disrespectful communicator, doesn't allow feelings to be expressed.
4. You're overreacting. Not act that way and neither should you.
5. Conclusion-end of discussion.
   Luminita: This shuts someone down and breaks trust of sharing future feelings, opinions or beliefs.

6. That's ridiculous!
    This dismisses one's opinion, feelings, or point of view
7. That's silly.
    This is a shutdown phrase. Killer of thoughts, hopes, dreams, beliefs, worries, stress, sadness or joys.
8. You're making a big deal out of nothing!
    Luminita: Haven't we all heard that at one time or another? Author says that this is another attempt to share their own personal point of view and opinion down their spouse's throat. Just because something does not matter to them does not mean that it is not a big, huge "something" to their spouse. It's not other's right to talk their partner out of their emotions.
9. That's not my problem.
    This is completely contradictory to being in a relationship. One must care about what happens in their partner's life. It does not mean they can solve all their partner's problems, but they can be listeners and empathetic.

Prayer

Hollywood, help me out pray for your fellow stars, for their salvation and to come off drugs for those who use them and off alcohol.

Dining Out

Hollywood, please pay your tabs at restaurants. Some of you do not pay your bill, only requesting to put it on your tab, mounting up to thousands of dollars, frustrating restaurant owners. Let's be civil please! They work hard to prepare your food and to serve you expensive food and drinks.

Is It Sin To:

Walk around your home naked in front of your housekeeper, butler, children, siblings, or whomever it may be?

Yes, it is sin, "You shall not uncover the nakedness of your father, you shall not uncover the nakedness of your mother, you shall not uncover the nakedness of your sister, you shall not uncover the nakedness of your son's daughter or of your daughter's daughter, of your father's wife's daughter, the nakedness of your mother's sister, your father's brother or his wife, your daughter in law for she is your son's wife or your brother's wife," Leviticus 18:7-16.

Now let's get into the birds and the bees.
Love Making

Let love making be natural, with man being in dominance, as God left it, no indecent acts. Also, no sex toys.

Telephone Sex Lines

Do not call telephone sex lines and do not watch sex videos neither. It is all sinful. Masturbation is sin also.

Multiple Partners

If there are any in Hollywood practicing these, they are sin. No orgies!

Sexless Friendships

Friends are not supposed to know each other sexually. Sex is for married couples only. Sexless friendships are the best, and they are clean friendships. Do not invite your female friend over for love when your husband leaves for work. Do not have lesbian friendships or homosexual friendships or even heterosexual friendships. Get married and have just one sexual partner: your spouse. This is the only sex instituted and permitted by God and this is marital sex.

Forbidden Lovemaking
1. Do not make love while spouse has menstrual cycle, neither at the beginning or end of cycle. The cycle must be completely over. Not many people practice this.
2. Do not make love immediately after childbirth. A uterus takes up to six weeks to close up completely, after which love-making can resume.

3. Do not make love while there are unresolved offenses. Doing so adds more resentment to the marriage relationship.

Me Too Movement

Knowing that a man has a much stronger sex drive, I will never meet with one alone again, nor dress seductively at the office. Hope no one finds out about my shame.

Me Too Movement

The one who has the slit in her dress all the way to her thigh is the one who screams Me Too the loudest.

Nomophobia-Fear of being without your mobile phone. We've all been there. If we find ourselves without it, what do we do? We can flag people down or ask to use someone else's phone, if they have one. No panic.

Ladies, checkout Trendsgal.com!

Wives Saved by Childbirth

"Wives will be saved in childbearing if they continue in faith, love and holiness, with selfcontrol," 1 Timothy 2:15.

This Scripture means that all wives must have children in order to attain salvation, unless one is barren.

RUNNING WITH ENDURANCE by Charles Stanley

A marathon is a taxing race. The runner must overcome muscle cramps, blisters, and the urge to quit. But each step reaffirms his commitment to keep going until he triumphantly crosses the finish line.

In many ways, this is what the Christian life is like. It's not a fast sprint to heaven but a long, obedient marathon. There are obstacles that could cause us to stumble and burdens we need to lay aside, so we can run unencumbered. The one word that summarizes our earthly race is endurance. This term implies going through something difficult without quitting. It includes the concept of abiding under hardships with patient, sustaining perseverance. Christ hasn't promised us an easy life.

In fact He told His disciples, "In the world, you will have tribulation," John 16:33.

How can we keep going? The answer is to fix our eyes on Jesus, not on the hardships and obstacles in our life. He set the pattern for us by enduring the cross for the joy set before Him. To focus on the must read the Scriptures. Then we'll be able to see what He would have us do, how we're to respond to various situations in life, which resources He's provided to help us, and what He has promised us at the finish line.

The joy set before us includes an imperishable, undefiled inheritance reserved for us in Heaven, 1 Peter 1:4, and an eternal weight of glory far beyond comparison to our earthly sufferings, 2 Corinthians 4:17. But best of all, when we finally cross the finish line, we will enter into presence to be with Him forever.

I am commenting on certain phrases in Stanley's article:

Stanley wrote that we endure and go through difficult times and hardships with perseverance. I relate these words to my marriage of ten years. These words are powerful to me, being in a dual religion and dual culture marriage, with my husband conflicting and opposing my faith and showing dislikes for certain cultural differences. I was jolted many times and was thrust into deep, lamentation by these oppressions and felt alone and helpless many times. I felt misunderstood by my husband, who was not a practicing Christian, nor a Church attendant as my children and I were.

We also read that "an eternal weight of glory awaits us. "I have seen the crown of many saints and they are glorious. I have seen the saints up in heaven shining like the sun and have experienced the presence of God and Jesus Christ. I was taken to Heaven in a dream and was shown certain kinds of worship and experienced the atmosphere of Heaven and God's presence. It is a presence we want to be in eternally, forever and ever and ever! We must do everything we can to enter the Kingdom of Heaven, a place full of God's glory and splendor which cannot be described.

Gurus

In Hinduism and Buddhism is a spiritual leader, especially one who imparts initiation. He is a teacher, a counselor, a mentor, leader, master.

Christians should not counsel with Gurus as they are not led by the Holy Spirit. They do not possess the Holy Spirit and will lead you astray. Much of their advice is demonic, false, speculative, and delusional.

Facebook Post by David Platt:

"We desperately need to explore how much of our understanding of the Gospel is American and how much is Biblical."

Biblical Mandate: Head Veil-Women and the Veil

1. Veil-not a cultural thing but a Biblical Mandate: Propriety In Worship

   Women are mandated by God to wear a veil, "The head of every man is Christ, and the head of the woman is man, and the head of Christ is God. Every man who prays or prophesies with his head covered dishonors his head. And every woman who prays or prophesies with her head uncovered dishonors her head-it is just as if her head were shaved. If a woman does not cover her head, she should have her hair cut off, and if it a disgrace for a woman to have her hair cut off or shaved off, she should have her head covered. A man ought not to cover his head since he is the image and glory of God, but the woman is the glory of man. For man did not come from woman but woman from man; neither was man created for woman but woman for man. For this reason and because of the angel's sake, the woman ought to have a sign of authority on her head," 1 Corinthians 11:3-10.

   So many times, when we see women who are veiled, it could be a religious thing for them and not a cultural thing. Many Americans associate head covering with outside cultures, but for many, it is a Biblical thing to cover the head. American women have to cover their heads, too, should they desire to follow Jesus Christ and the teachings of the Bible. It is not an un-American thing to veil your head, it is a Biblical Mandate. I veil my head in Church and at home when I pray or do intense Bible study. Some women wear it always, but I was not raised that way. I wear it where it is called for.

Proper Church Wear

Hollywood, please wear proper attire in the Church: no miniskirts, shorts, see-through clothes, gowns with slits up to the thigh, no cleavage, no dresses with exposed backs, no string dresses or tops, no sleeveless gowns or tops, off-the-shoulder blouses or dresses, and no belly button exposing t-shirts. The Church is the House of the Living God, and it needs to be respected.

Do Good Works Save Me?

Many people do a lot of good works and believe this earns them salvation. Good works are essential for salvation, but one must do a lot more to enter the Kingdom of God. There is a Salvation Process to follow. Let's go into this salvation process:

The Salvation Process

1. Believe and Confess

    "If you confess with your mouth the Lord Jesus and believe in your heart that God raised Him from the dead, you shall be saved. For with the heart man believes unto righteousness, and with the mouth confession is made unto salvation," Romans 10:9-10.

2. Repent

    "Repent ye therefore converted, that your sins may be blotted out, that times of refreshing may come from the Lord," Acts 3:19.

3. Confession of Sins

   "If we confess our sins, He is faithful and just to forgive us our sins and to cleanse us from all unrighteousness," 1 John 1:9.

4. Holy Spirit Baptism

   "Ye shall receive power when the Holy Spirit is come upon you, and you shall be witnesses unto Me in Jerusalem, and in all Judea, and in Samaria and to the uttermost part of it," Acts 1:8.

5. Water Baptism

   "Repent and be baptized everyone of you in the Name of Jesus Christ for the remission of sins, and ye shall receive the gift of the Holy Ghost," Acts 2:38.

6. The Lord's Supper

   "The Lord Jesus, the same night in which He was betrayed took bread, and when He had given thanks, He broke it and said, 'Take, eat, this is My body which is broken for you; do this in remembrance of Me.' After the same manner, He also took the cup, when He had supped saying, 'This cup is the New Testament in My blood, this do ye as often as ye drink it, in remembrance of Me. For as often as ye eat this bread and drink this cup, ye do show the Lord's death till He comes," 1 Corinthians 11:23-26.

7. Feet Washing

   "Before the Feast of the Passover, when Jesus knew that His hour was come that He should depart out of this world unto the Father, having loved His own which were in the world, He loved them unto the end. He rose from the Supper, laid aside His garments, and took a towel and girded Himself. After that, He poured water into a basin and began to wash His disciples' feet, and to wipe them with the towel with which He was girded. Then Jesus said, 'Know ye what I have done to you? Ye call Me Master and Lord, and ye de well, for so am I.

If I then, your Lord and Master, have washed your feet, ye also ought to wash one another's feet. for I have given you an example, that ye should do as I have done to you. Verily, verily, I say unto you, the servant is not greater than His Lord, neither is he that is sent greater than he that sent him. If ye know these things, happy are ye if ye do them," John 13:1-17.

The Lords Supper and Feet Washing are two major Ordinances of the Church which must be practiced by Christians.

8. Alms-Giving to The Poor

    "Now concerning the collection for the saints, as I directed the Churches of Galatia, so do you also. On the first day of every week, each one of you is to put aside and save, as he may prosper," 1 Corinthians 16:1-3. And, "Instruct them to do good, to be rich in good works, to be generous and ready to share," 1 Timothy 6:18.

9. Tithing-Giving to The Church

    "This I say, He who sows sparingly shall also reap sparingly; and he who sows bountifully shall also reap bountifully. Every man according as he purposes in his heart, so let him give, not grudgingly or of necessity, for God loves a cheerful giver. And God is able to make all grace abound toward you that ye, always having all sufficiency in all things, may abound to every good work. 2 Corinthians 9:6-8.

    The Church of today usually follow the pattern of the Israelites, the Mosaic Law on tithing, "One tenth of the produce of the land, whether grain from the fields, or fruit from the trees, belongs to the Lord and must be set apart to Him as holy," Leviticus 27:30. So, this is 10% of one's income, which must be tithed to the Church.

10. Praise and Worship God

    "Let everything that has breath praise the Lord," Psalm 150:6. "God is a Spirit and those that worship Him must worship Him in truth and in Spirit," Ephesians 4:24.

Three Major Theological False Teachings Taking America To Hell

1. Born Again Doctrine

   This is the belief that one is born again when they pray a prayer of salvation. But to be born again, one must be born of the water and of the Spirit, John 3:5. To be born of water means to 'be baptized in water for the remission of sins', Mark 1:4. And to be born of the Spirit means to 'be Baptized in the Holy Spirit', Acts 2:1-4. So you need the baptism in water and the baptism in the Holy Spirit to be born again. Without these two baptisms, one cannot be saved. A mere prayer does not save you. These two baptisms are a must in order to be saved. Hollywood, seek these two baptisms.

   You also need to make a confession of sins, "If we confess our sins, He is faithful and just to forgive us our sins and to cleanse us of all unrighteousness," 1 John 1:9. There's more steps to take to be saved in the Salvation Process above.

2. Holy Spirit Baptism

   Many believe they have received the Holy Spirit when they were baptized as babies, others believe they received Him at the prayer of salvation. Both are false. In the Book of Acts Chapter 2:1-4, we are told that the Holy Spirit is power and its evidence is speaking in tongues. One needs to be delivered of evil spirits first and then be baptized in the Holy Spirit, which cannot be mistaken with anything on earth as it enters the heart with great power. If you have not experienced this great power entering your heart, then you did not receive the Holy Spirit. Everyone who does not have the Spirit is possessed by evil spirits and should seek Jesus Christ who gives the Spirit freely, John 1:33-34.

3. The Endtimes: Pre-Tribbers

   Many believe in a Pre-Tribulation Rapture which means that Christians will not have part in the Great Tribulation, but Let's see what the Word of God says about this, "For then shall be such great tribulation such as was not since the beginning of the world to this time, no, nor ever shall be. And except those days should be shortened, there should no flesh be saved; but for the elect's sake, those days shall be shortened," Matthew 24:21-22.

This Scripture proves that Christians will go through the Tribulation. We are God's elect as we are called in verse 22.

Here is another Scripture in Matthew 24, which proves Christians, called the Elect, will go through the Great Tribulation, "Immediately after the Tribulation of those days, shall the sun be darkened and the moon shall not give her light and the stars shall fall from heaven; and the powers of the heavens shall be shaken. And then shall appear the sign of the Son of Man in heaven; and then shall all the tribes of the earth mourn, and they shall see the Son of Man coming in the clouds of heaven with power and great glory. And He shall send His angels with a great sound of a trumpet, and they shall gather together His elect from the four winds, from the end of heaven to the other," Matthew 24:29-31. Let's skip to verses 36 to 42, "But of that day and hour no man knows, no, not the angels of heaven, but My Father only. But as the days of Noah were, so shall also the coming of the Son of Man be. For as in the days that were before the flood, they were eating and drinking, marrying and giving in marriage, until the day that Noah entered into the Ark. And they did not know until the flood came and took them all away, so shall also the coming of the Son of Man be. Then shall two be in the field; the one shall be taken and the other left. Two women shall be grinding at the mill; the one shall be taken and the other left. Watch therefore for ye know not what hour your Lord comes. When one is taken and one is left, this is called the Rapture, also called The Coming of the Son of Man."

Big Bang Theory

The Big Bang Theory states that the universe was formed about fourteen billion years ago as the result of a giant explosion of very dense and hot matter. This matter expanded and started to cool down, going through different transitional phases. The universe has been expanding ever since. This is the Scientific Theory of Creationism. Let's see what the Bible says about Creationism.

"In the beginning, God created the heavens and the earth. The earth was without form and void, and darkness was on the face of the deep. And the Spirit of God was hovering over the face of the waters. Then God said 'Let there be light.' And there was light. God called the Light Day and the Darkness He called Night. So the evening and the morning were the first day," Genesis 1:1-5. God created the earth through commands. Christians believe the Bible version of the creation of the earth, not the scientific version. If one does not believe the Bible, he is not a Christian because Christians believe the Bible. The Bible is supreme over all other books in the world.

Me Too Movement

Women unintentionally put themselves at risk of assault by provocative wear, exposing too much skin, by beautifying themselves exceedingly with hair dyes, makeup or too much makeup, made up nails, and seductive eyes with long lashes or fake eye lashes and heavy lipstick. This is enticing to men. Ladies may say that upkeeping themselves this way is just a part of life, but this does not change the fact that they are tempting to men.

Me Too Movement

No more showing cleavage at the office or anywhere! In today's society, women's breasts are perceived as lovemaking assets. Women's breasts are for babies and are not to be seen by men. Showing cleavage and legs is very sinful, punishable by hell, lest one repents. God warns us about causing others to sin.

"Whoever causes one of these little ones who believe in Me to sin, it would be better for the one to have a great millstone fastened around the neck and to be drawn in the depths of the sea," Mark 9:42. Yes, it is sin to entice, seduce, and tempt men, even if it's unintentional.

And it's very sinful also for men to rape, assault women, and is punishable by hell, lest one repents.

Men and women, God demands that we conquer temptation, "There has no temptation taken you but such as is common to man: but God is faithful who will not suffer you to be tempted above that ye are able, but will with the temptation also make a way of escape, that ye may be able to bear it," 1 Corinthians 10:13. So men, pray to beat temptation. Do not yield to sexual temptation and rape or assault anyone.

Twerking is sinful, degrading, and repulsive. Stop it.
Me Too Movement

A law should be passed where a woman will not be permitted to wear on the job: short skirts, skin-tight skirts, skirts with high slits in them revealing legs, see-through blouses, or exposing cleavage. This distracts men and is tempting to them. This kind of conduct by women provokes adultery and/or rapes and in many cases breaks marriages apart. I make a note here that not all women who are assaulted are provocatively dressed.

Seven People Everyone Needs in Their Life by Beliefnet
1. Mentor: To glean experience and advice from; trusted counsel in career and spiritual journey and relationships.
2. Encourager: They say, "I believe in you."
3. Tough Love Giver: Stops you from a destructive path.
4. Dream Builder: Will inspire you to make your dreams happen.
5. Keeper of Secrets: Will guard your reputation.
6. Mercy Releasers: Shows forgiveness and are optimistic on things.
7. Loyal Friend: Wholeheartedness and dedication: loves you through good times and bad
times-always there for you.

Me Too Movement

I will never flirt with a man again, for I fear I could be shamed again.

Scientology

Ron Hubbard-Founder of Scientology

Scientology means "the study of truth." It exists to provide help, help for all people at every strata of life, of every disability or ability and across all ethnic and religious boundaries. Born out of this desire to help are many social betterment activities Scientology supports. From our education programs, providing real answers to declining literacy levels to our solutions for criminal support and drug rehabilitation. Everything we do in Scientology is in the name of "help."

L. Ron Hubbard said, "The world is carried on the backs of a desperate few. It is this desperate few who are often the most neglected."

It is for this reason that Hubbard saw to the formation of a Special Church of Scientology, which would cater to these individuals: the artists, politicians, leaders of industry, sports figures, and anyone with the power and vision to create a better world. That Church is "Celebrity Centre International."

Luminita: Adherents to this religion must come out of it or they will perish. There is no truth in it. God is not in it. Salvation is only through Jesus Christ.

He is the world's only Savior, "Nor is there salvation in any other, for there is no other Name under heaven given among men by which we must be saved," Acts 4:12.

Did you know?

Did you know Jesus was a Carpenter on earth?

Racism: Charlottesville Protests

Here is a letter I sent to CNN concerning the Charlottesville Protests:

August 12th, 2018

I regret the protests in Charlottesville by White Nationalists and am sorry for Heather, who was killed a year ago in a similar protest. I hope this nation can achieve some sort of racial unity, acceptance, and tolerance. And my message to White Nationalists is to repent. Stop all racism and racial superiority. God created us all equal. God will judge those who cause divisions, dissensions, and violence in this nation. Repent to God and seek His forgiveness.

If there are any White Nationalists in Hollywood, cease to be one! Love your fellow humans regardless of color.

Racist Federal Monuments

Another letter I sent to CNN:

All federal monuments, which promote racial superiority should be taken down.

Marriage is Sacred and Binding

"Furthermore, it has been said, 'Whoever divorces his wife, let him give her a certificate of divorce. But I say to you that whoever divorces his wife for any reason except sexual immorality causes her to commit adultery; and whoever marries a woman who is divorced commits adultery," Matthew 5:31-32.

This Scripture forbids divorced people to marry other people, regardless of sexual immorality (if one spouse committed adultery).

Jesus Forbids Oaths

"Again you have heard that it was said to of old, 'You shall not swear falsely, but shall perform your oaths to the Lord. But I say to you do not swear at all: neither by heaven, for it is God's Throne, nor by the earth for it is His footstool, nor by Jerusalem for it is the city of the Great King. Nor shall you swear by your head, because you cannot make one hair white or black. But let your "Yes" be Yes and your "No" be No. For whatever is more than these is from the evil one," Matthew 5:33-36.

Love Poem

The Gucci clothesThe expensive jewelry
The big, fancy house
The eye-catching Lamborghini
The fat bank account
Too much it does not account
If your love for me does not truly abound
These things are only temporary
They're not the things I truly need
What I truly need is you
Spend time with me
In your arms you cuddle me
Exalt me to all
And your love will make me bawl
Honor me
And forever with you I will be
Communicate with me
And one we will be
Promise from being faithful, you will not abate
This way I I'll not be ashamed
Always adore me
And forever you will keep me.

Me Too Movement

Coerced Sex

Anchorwoman was told she was too pretty not to give in.

Do Aliens Really Exist?

Yes, they are, "Spiritual hosts of wickedness in the heavenly places," Ephesians 6:12.

The Bible tells about demonic powers, "For we do not wrestle against flesh and blood, but against principalities, against powers, against rulers of the darkness of this age, against spiritual hosts of wickedness in the heavenly places," Ephesians 6:12.

If anyone has seen aliens or apparitions in the air, they are the demonic powers of the air far up in the sky; the Bible calls it "in the heavens." They are not friendly beings. They are of the Satan's kingdom. They are evil and wreck much havoc on earth and in the nature. They are not to be admired or invited to earth as some do by saying, "Welcome" or "Come to Earth" or "We love you." They are very powerful and can destroy people and do all kinds of wickedness upon earth.

You Cannot Serve God and Mammon

"No one can serve two masters; for either he will hate the one and love the other; or he will be loyal to the one and despise the other. You cannot serve God and Mammon," Matthew 6:24.

"Mammon" means money. You can have riches and much money as long as you serve the Lord with it. Do not set your heart on money.

Wikipedia: Horoscopes

A horoscope is an astrological chart or diagram representing the positions of the Sun, Moon, Planets, astrological aspects, and sensitive angels at the time of an event, such as the moment of a person's birth.

The horoscope is used to tell fortune or other events in a person's life. It is sin to read, believe, and use the horoscope as a guide in life.

Wikipedia: Zodiac Signs

These are the astrological symbols/glyphs used in Western astrology to represent the astrological signs.

Wikipedia: Chinese Horoscopes

In Chinese astrology, horoscopes are based on the symbolism of the Chinese zodiac, a system of elements and animals associated with each year according to a Sexagenary cycle.

So, do not read or believe zodiac signs and horoscopes.

They are deceiving and misleading and the Bible opposes it, "And take heed, lest you raise your eyes to heaven, and when you see the sun, the moon, and the stars, all the hosts of heaven, you feel driven to worship them and to serve them, which the Lord your God has given to all the peoples under the whole heaven as a heritage," Deuteronomy 4:19.

Hollywood, you may not bow down and worship the sun, moon, and stars, but you serve them by believing in horoscopes and zodiac signs and your birth sign, such as Aquarius, Cancer, Libra, Sagitarious, etc. Abandon all these things, even your birthstone. All these things are rooted in demonic religions and cultures.

Satanism

Satanism is a group of ideological and philosophical beliefs based on Satan. Stars who attend Satan's Temples or Churches should stop. And all who have made a pact with Satan should confess their sins to God and seek His forgiveness. God can lift the curse of Satan off you and make you His children.

Do not embrace images of Satan occult practices, or attend Satanic functions anymore. Satan is our adversary, not our friend.

Me Too Movement

There is one of my male co-workers at the door to visit. I will not open the door.

"You have to come back later when my husband will be home."
Catholicism: Halloween

Halloween, also known as Allhallowtide, began as the time in the liturgical year dedicated to remembering the dead, including those in purgatory, dead saints, martyrs, and all the faithful departed. Its roots are in Catholicism, a dammed religion which no one can be saved through, and a religion which added many false doctrines, beliefs, and practices to true Christianity. Halloween in itself is demonic and Christians ought not to acknowledge or celebrate it.

God Hates Halloween
The Bible Condemns These Practices
1.   Witches: Exodus 22:18
     "Thou shall not suffer a witch to live."

2. Vampires: Leviticus 7:26-27

" Moreover, ye shall eat no manner of blood, whether it be of fowl or beast, in any of your dwellings. Whatsoever soul it be that eats any manner of blood, even that soul shall be cut off from his people."

3. Wizards: Deuteronomy 18:10-12

"There shall not be found anyone among you that makes his son or his daughter to pass through the fire, or that uses divination, or an observer of times, or an enchanter, or a witch. Or a charmer, or a consulter with familiar spirits, or a wizard, or a necromancer (a practice of magic, communicating with the dead-either by summoning their spirits as apparitions or raising them bodily for the purpose of divination, imparting the means to foretell future events, discover hidden knowledge, to bring someone back from the dead or to use the dead as a weapon. For all that do these things are an abomination unto the Lord: and because of these abominations the Lord thy God drives you out from before Him."

4. Ghosts: Leviticus 19:31

"Regard not them that have familiar spirits, neither seek after wizards, to be defiled by them: I am the Lord your God."

Me Too Movement

At the office, I didn't feel this way, but being alone with him at the private meeting, things suddenly changed. Now I must endure the pain and shame.

Forgiveness

"For if you forgive men their trespasses, your Heavenly Father will also forgive you. But if you do not forgive men their trespasses, neither will your Father forgive you your trespasses," Matthew 6:14-15.

This means that if we do not forgive, God cannot forgive us, which will keep us from attaining our salvation. So we must forgive, let go of all grudges, all hate, all vengeance, and all resentments and try to love our offenders.

Hollywood, forgive Harvey Weinstein so he, too, can enter the pearly gates of heaven with you. He did not commit all the assaults in this book. Only one assault, although he had many accusers. And while you're at it, forgive Epstein also and Larry Nasser and all the Moonves's.

More Scriptures on Forgiveness

"Let all bitterness and wrath, and anger, and clamour and evil speaking be put away from you, with all malice. And be ye kind one to another, tenderhearted, forgiving one another, even as God for Christ's sake has forgiven you," Ephesians 4:31-32.

"Take heed to yourselves: If thy brother trespass against thee, rebuke him and if he repents, forgive him. And if he trespasses against thee seven times in a day, and seven times in a day turn again to thee saying, I repent, thou shall forgive him," Luke 17:3-4.

Hollywood: Star Competitions

Let's stop all competitions, Hollywood. Do not quarrel about who has the best hair, dress, biceps, legs, and so on. Who has natural blue eyes, is best dressed, who makes the most money, who has the most Emmys, Awards, etc. Try to share stardom in quietness and in friendship with one another.

Bible Quiz

If any man be in Christ, he is
a new creation
full of blessing
a righteous man
heavenly minded
Answer: 2 Corinthians 5:17

Abiding in God

1. Walk In Love

   "Therefore, be imitators of God as dear children and walk in love as Christ also loved us and given Himself for us, an offering and a sacrifice to God for a sweet-smelling aroma. But fornication and all uncleanness or covetousness, let it not even be named among you, as is fitting for saints; neither filthiness nor foolish talking, nor course jesting, which are not fitting, but rather giving of thanks. For this you know, that no fornicator, unclean person, nor covetous man, who is an idolater, has any inheritance in the Kingdom of Christ and God. Let no one deceive you with empty words, for because of these things the wrath of God comes upon the sons of disobedience. Therefore, do not be partakers with them," Ephesians 5:1-7.

   This Scripture tells us to avoid these sins and even those who commit them.

2. Walk in Light

   " For you were once darkness, but now you are light in the Lord. Walk as children of light. For the fruit of the Spirit is in all goodness, righteousness and truth, finding out what is acceptable to the Lord. And have no fellowship with the unfruitful works of darkness, but rather expose them," Ephesians 5:8-11.

   This Scripture means to have nothing to do with evil but rather expose evil. It means to expose people who do evil!

3. Walk in Wisdom

   " See then that you walk circumspectly, not as fools, but as wise, redeeming the times, because the days are evil. Therefore, do not be unwise, but understand what the will of the Lord is. And do not be drunk with wine in which is dissipation, but be filled with the Spirit, speaking to one another in psalms, and hymns and spiritual songs, singing and making melody in your heart to the Lord; giving thanks always for all things to God the Father in the Name of our Lord Jesus Christ, submitting to one another in the fear of God," Ephesians 5:16-21.

"Redeeming the time" means to use your time wisely, doing the works of God and not evil things or doing your thing only.

Lying: Do Not Grieve The Holy Spirit

"Therefore, putting away lying, let each one of you speak truth with his neighbor, for we are members of one Body," Ephesians 4:25.

When people lie, they grieve (hurt, sadden) the Holy Spirit. "Being members of one body" means that all Christians who are being saved are members of the Body of Christ.

Quote
"Read your Bible. It is our manual for daily living. It brings eternal life, salvation to the soul."
Luminita Dragu

Did You Know?

Did you know that Jesus hung on the cross for six hours? Mark 15:25.

Calling of The Rich

"Command those who are rich in this present age not to be haughty, nor to trust in uncertain riches, but in the living God, who gives us richly all things to enjoy. Let them do good, that they be rich in good works, ready to give, willing to share, storing up for themselves a good foundation for the time to come, that they may lay hold on eternal life," 1 Timothy 6:17-19.

Did You Know?

Did you know Kim Kardashian's whole name is Kimberly Noel Kardashian?

Catholicism: Baby Baptism

Babies do not need to be baptized-their heads sprinkled with water. This is an addition to the Catholic religion-another false teaching. The only water baptism the Bible tells us to follow is the Baptism of Jesus. Jesus got baptized to fulfill all righteousness, John 3:15. We get baptized when we are of age of right and wrong and when we can commit fully to Jesus Christ and to His service. The Water Baptism is a Covenant we make with God to live a holy life, to follow Him all the days of our lives. It is a baptism of repentance, Mark 1:4, Acts 2:38.

The Water Baptism also comes with confession of sins, "And they were baptized by Him in the Jorden River, confessing their sins," Matthew 3:6. Babies have to wait till they are of a mature age, at least eighteen, so they can make this Covenant with God on their own. God does not receive babies' baptisms. He rejects them and these babies grow up and perish unless they get baptized in water at a mature age and follow Christ all the days of their lives.

Wikipedia: Amal Clooney Biography

Aural Alamuddin Clooney, a lawyer, activist, born in 1978, has a distinguished career focused on International Law and Human Rights Issues. She is married to zctor George Clooney.

The Lebanese-British lawyer was born in Beirut in 1978 and raised in England. She studied at Oxford University and NYU before beginning her notable law career. Along with her high-profile defense cases, Amal has been a part of several United Nations Commissions and Tribunals and lectured at top universities. In 2014, she married superstar actor George Clooney, with whom she has twins.

Amal Ramzi Alamuddin was born in Beirut on February 3rd, 1978. Her father was a professor at the American University in Beirut and owner of a travel agency. Her mother was a journalist. When Amal was two-years-old, her family fled Lebanon to escape the ravages of the Civil War that had begun in the mid 1970's and engulfed the country in violence.

The family settled in London, England in 1980. Amal earned a scholarship at Oxford University. While there she developed an interest in human rights before graduating with a Bachelor's degree in Law in 2000.

Amal Alamuddin then entered the NYU of Law to pursue a Master's degree. Amal has worked at the US Court of Appeals with future Supreme Court Justice Sonya Sotomayor and at the International Court of Justice.

In 2005, Alamuddin refocused her career on International Law when she became part of a United Nations Tribunal established to prosecute the persons responsible for the assassination of former Lebanese Prime Minister Rafic Hariri. Amal went on to handle several high-profile cases in International Courts, including the defense of former Ukranian Prime Minister Yulia Tymoshenko, Muammar al-Qadaffi's intelligence Airel Abdullah al-Senussi, and WikiLeaks Editor-in-Chief Julian Assange.

Philanthropy

Amal Clooney is the President of the Clooney Foundation for Justice, which she co-founded with her husband George Clooney in late 2016 to advance justice in courtrooms, communities, and classrooms around the world.

Amal partnered with the Aurora Humanitarian Initiative in beginning the Amal Clooney Scholarship, which was created to send one female student from Lebanon to the United World College Dilijan each year, to enroll in a two-year International Baccalaureate (IB) program.

Amal Clooney and her husband sponsor a Yazidi student, Hazim Avdal, who Amal met via her work with Nadia Murad as Avdal worked at Yazda. He is attending the University of Chicago.

Orphan Poem

Amal in your busy schedule
Might you have time for me too
I don't require much for you to do

67

I'm an orphan and need your help too
On me can you spend a dollar or two
We are the orphans of the world
We need the help of the whole world

Amal, will you open your heart to orphans and help them? You can find many orphan causes in the US and even around the world. I will participate in this cause by matching your giving up to $100,000.

Wikipedia: George Clooney Biography

George Timothy Clooney (born May 6th, 1961) is an American actor and businessman. He is the recipient of three Golden Globe Awards and two Academy Awards: one for acting in Syriana (2006) and one for co-producing 92012. In 2018, he was the recipient of the AFI Live Achievement Award at the age of fifty-seven.

In 2009, Clooney was included in "Time's Annual Time 100" as one of the most influential people in the world. He is also noted for his political and economic activism and has served as one of the United Nations Messengers of Peace on January 31st, 2008. He is also a member of the Council on Foreign Relations.

Clooney's mother, Nina Bruce, was a beauty queen and city councilwoman. His father, Nick Clooney, is a former anchorman and television host, including five years on the AMC Network.

Clooney is of Irish, German, and English ancestry. His maternal great-great-great-great-grandmother, Mary Ann Sparrow, was the half-sister of Nancy Lincoln, mother of President Abraham Lincoln. Clooney has an older sister named Adelia known as Ada. Cabaret singer and actress Rosemary Clooney was an aunt to Clooney. Through Rosemary his cousins include actors Miguel Ferrer, Rafael Ferrer, and Gabriel Ferrer, who is married to Debby Boone.

George Clooney is Roman Catholic. He attended Northern Kentucky University from 1979 to 1981, majoring in broadcast journalism, and very briefly attended the University of Cincinnati. He earned money selling women's shoes, insurance door-to-door, stocking shelves, working in construction, and cutting tobacco.

Clooney rose to fame when he played Dr. Doug Ross alongside Anthony Edwards, Juliana Margulies, and Noah Wyle on the hit NBC medical drama ER from 1994 to 1999. For his work on the series, Clooney received two Primetime Emmy Award Nominations for Outstanding Lead Actor in a Drama Series in 1995 and 1996. He also earned three Golden Globe Award nominations for Best Actor-Television Series Drama in 1995, 1996, and 1997 (losing to co-star Anthony Edwards).

Clooney began appearing in films while working on ER. His first major Hollywood role was in the honor comedy-thriller, From Dusk to Dawn, the romantic comedy, One Fine Day, and the action thriller, The Peacemaker.

Clooney has too many films to mention them all. I say he has big success on the screen.

Activism and Public Advocacy

Actor George Clooney supported both of Barack Obama's 2008 and 2012 presidential campaigns. He is a supporter of gay rights. in 2016, Clooney endorsed Hillary Clinton for the 2016 Presidential Election.

Humanitarian Works

George Clooney is involved in the "Not on Our Watch Project," an organization that focuses global attention and resources to stop and prevent mass atrocities, along with Brad Pitt, Matt Damon, Don Cheadle, David Pressman, and Jerry Weintraub. In 2010, he organized the telethon "Hope for Haiti Now," which collected donations for the 2010 Haiti earthquake victims.

Same-Sex Marriage

In March 2012, Clooney, with Martin Sheen and Brad Pitt, were featured in a performance of Dustin Lance Black's Play "8," a staged re-enactment of the federal trial that overturned California's Proposal 8 Ban on same-sex marriage, as attorney David Boies. This production helped raise money for the American Foundation for Equal Rights.

LGBT

In 2012, Clooney offered to take an auction winner to lunch to benefit the Gay, Lesbian, and Straight Education Network (GLSEN) works to create a safe space in school for children who are or may be perceived to be gay, lesbian, bi-sexual, or transgender.

World Conflicts

George Clooney has advocated a resolution of the Darfur Conflict. He spoke at a 2006, "Save Darfur" Rally in Washington, DC. In April 2006, he spent ten days in Chad and Sudan with his father to make the TV Special "A Journey to Darfur," reflecting the situation of Darfur's Refugees and advocated for action.

Armenian Genocide

George Clooney is a keen supporter of the recognition of the Armenian Genocide. He is one of the chief associates of the "100 Lives Initiatives," a project which aims to remember the lives lost during the event. As part of the Initiative, Clooney launched the Aurora Prize, which awards to those who risk their lives to prevent genocides and atrocities. Clooney had also urged various American government officials to support the US Recognition of the Armenian Genocide. Clooney visited Armenia to commemorate the 101st anniversary of the event in April 2016.

Wikipedia: The Armenian Genocide also known as The Armenian Holocaust was the Ottoman government's systematic extermination of 1.5 million Armenians, mostly citizens within the Ottoman Empire. On April 24th, 1915, the Ottoman authorities rounded up, arrested, and deported from Constantinople (now Istanbul) to the region of Ankana, 235 to 270 Armenian Intellectuals and community leaders, the majority of whom were eventually murdered.

The Genocide was carried out during and after World War I and implemented in two phases: the wholesale killing of the able-bodies male population through massacre and subjection of army conscripts to forced labor, followed by deportation of women, children, the elderly, and the infirm of death marches leading to the Syrian Desert. Driven forward by military escorts, the deportees were deprived of food and water and subjected periodic robbery, rape, and massacre. Most Armenian diaspora communities around the world came into being as a direct result of the Genocide. The motive for this Genocide is anti-Armenian sentiments.

As I have always said, "Racism is the biggest demon attacking humanity." Racism takes away the peace among humanity from nations. It is behind many wars, genocides, and atrocities.

So we see that George and Amal are very different people, yet they are similar in the work they do. Somehow fate has found them in different parts of the world and has put them together through marriage.

Gun Control

In 2018, following the Stoneman Douglas High School Shooting, the Clooney's pledged 500,000 to the "March For Our Lives" and said they would be in attendance.

Bible Quiz

What is deceitful above all things and desperately wickedno man can know?

Satan

Man's Governments

Satanism

The heart

Answer: Jeremiah 17:9

Catholicism: Purgatory

Purgatory is believed to be a place people go after death to pay for all their sins and then be received into Heaven. This is a false teaching of the Catholic religion.

The Bible tells us that, "It is appointed to men once to die, then comes judgment," Hebrews 9:27. No one can be forgiven of their sins after death. They are either ready to meet God or they are not. People are supposed to deal with their sins and make peace with God through Jesus Christ before death. Hollywood, come out of Catholicism. Do not pray for the dead anymore. Purgatory does not exist. There is only heaven and hell after death.

Catholicism: The Immaculate Heart of Mary

The Immaculate Heart of Mary is a devotional name used to refer to the internal life of the Blessed Virgin Mary; her joys and sorrows, her virtues and hidden perfections, and above all, her Virginal Love for God the Father, her maternal love for her son Jesus and her compassionate love for all people.

Yes, Mother Mary was a compassionate and loving person. And although we do esteem her very highly for she was the chosen one to bring the Son of God, Jesus, into the world to save humanity, but she was not sinless as the Roman Catholic portrays her and claims so. No man is without sin. "If we say we have no sins, we deceive ourselves and the truth is not in us," 1 John 1:8.

So all humanity needs the redemptive work of Jesus Christ, which He completed on the cross, including Mother Mary, who needed it and received it.

Plea For Salvation

"Have mercy upon me, Oh God,
According to Thy lovingkindness,
According unto the multitude of Thy tender mercies,
Blot out my transgressions
Wash me thoroughly from mine iniquity,
And cleanse me from my sin,
For I acknowledge my transgressions,
And my sin is ever before me,
Against thee, thee only, have I sinned,
Create in me a clean heart, O God,
And renew a right Spirit within me."
Psalm 51:1-10

Selena Gomez Kidney Complications

Selena Gomes was hospitalized again after having complications from the kidney transplant in 2018. She was observed by the medical team and is now back home and feeling well.

Hollywood Stars Triumphs/Achievements/Failures/Adversities

Kim Kardashian and Kanye West had their fourth child named Psalm West. Here are their other children's odd names: North West, Chicago West, and Saint West.

Kim Kardashian is an actress, a reality star, a model turning criminal lawyer.

Justin Bieber and Halley Baldwin tied the knot.

Beauty mogul Kylie Jenner sells $600 million stake in cosmetics company to Coty, a New York-based cosmetics company that also owns a number of international consumer beauty brands, including Cover Girl. The partnership will help Kylie's brand expand globally and enter new beauty categories.

In 2019, Jennifer Lopez was nominated by the Golden Globe as Best Supporting Actress.

Beyoncé won Grammy Award for Best Pop Solo Performance (2020-2017) She also won a Grammy Award for Best Urban Contemporary Album.

Hoda Kotb of the Today Show adopts a newborn son.

Kelly Clarkson started her own talk show. Every episode begins with her beautiful singing. Don't forget to tune in.

Tragedies and Adversities of Hollywood Stars

Nipsey Hussle dead (August 14th, 1985-March 31st, 2019)

Nipsey Hussle (Ermias Joseph Asghedom) was shot dead on March 31st, 2019 in south Los Angeles by twenty-nine-year-old Eric Holder, whom he had a confrontation with earlier in the day. He was an American rapper, entrepreneur, and community activist.

Selma Blair-Multiple Sclerosis

Selma Blair's adversity is her health battle with Multiple Sclerosis.

She revealed this diagnosis via Instagram on October 2018. Selma was born on June 23rd, 1972 in Southfield, Michigan (a Suburb of Detroit). Selma describes her disease as being debilitating with her at times, falling, dropping things, foggy. She promises to do her best with this illness, and I wish her the best indeed!

Prince George died of a drug overdose.

Model and Actress Kim Porter Dead at Forty-Seven

Model and Actress Kim Porter, who dated Rapper Diddy Combs, also known as Puff Daddy and Diddy Combs for thirteen years and is the mother of his three children, died in her Toluca Lake, California home. TMZ said Porter went into cardiac arrest after suffering from pneumonia for several weeks, though her official cause of death has not yet been revealed.

Bode Miller Family Tragedy: His nineteen-month-old baby girl, Emeline, drowned in a neighbor's pool. How tragic!

George and Amber Smith Family Tragedy: Their three-year-old son, River, has drowned in the family pool. How very tragic also! Let's keep these families in our prayers while they are going through this very difficult and traumatic time.

God's Phone Number

Psalm 50:15 – "Call upon Me in the day of trouble. I will deliver you, and you shall glorify Me."

Access Hollywood-Celebrity News

Jenna Bush Hager has a newborn son named Henry Harold Hager. Jenna has also joined the Today Show in early 2019.

Taylor Swift breaks Michael Jackson's record of Most-Ever American Music Awards.

Taylor Swift was also named the Artist of the Decade at the American Music Awards.

Kesha makes triumphant return to American Music Awards after a six-year absence.

Bible Quiz
Who is the head of Christ?
Man
Nobody, Christ is God
God
Christ Himself
Answer: 1 Corinthians 11:3

Me Too Movement
At his request, I privately met with him for business, and to my surprise, out the door he went, soon as he got the prize without consent. Letters Sent To CNN/Access Hollywood

I see into the lives of Hollywood stars through visions and mentor them as is needed. I also give them Biblical counsel when needed.

Attention CNN/Access Hollywood: Harvey Weinstein-December 16th, 2019

Harvey Weinstein has reached a tentative $44 million settlement in civil cases with women accusing him of sexual assault and harassment in US, Canada, and the United Kingdom. However, this is not enough. If Weinstein wishes to attain his salvation, he must acknowledge his fault in the sexual assaults of the women who are accusing him and must apologize to them. And the ladies must forgive Harvey as they to want forgiveness from God for their sins.

Scripture tells us, "Forbearing one another, and forgiving one another; If any man has a grievance against any, even as Christ forgave you, so also do ye," Collosians 3:13.

Attention CNN/Access Hollywood: Harry Potter-J.K. Rowling

The producer of Harry Potter, J.K. Rowling has infiltrated and poisoned the youth of this nation with witchcraft by producing the Harry Potter movie and the Harry Potter books, which contain witchcraft, magic, magic spells, and wizards. God is merciful and wishes to save. But for her to attain her salvation, she must apologize to the United

States for Harry Potter and not produce such movies anymore. Look what Scripture tells us about witchcraft:

"There shall not be found among you anyone that uses divination, or an observer of times, or an enchanter, or a witch, or a charmer, or a consulter with familiar spirits, or a wizard or a necromancer. For all that do these things are an abomination unto the Lord," Deuteronomy 18:10-12.

Attention CNN/Access Hollywood: September 10th, 2019-Justin Bieber Repentance

Justin Bieber made a public apology for his out of control lifestyle he had before he got married. He showed remorse for being a not so good role model at times. This is good for the youth of this nation. Wish more stars would do the same. God bless Bieber and his family.

Attention CNN/Access Hollywood: September 10th, 2019-Actress Selma Blair

I deeply regret having found out about your multiple sclerosis diagnosis. I am sorry that you are ill and disabled now. You may want to seek healing from God and also draw nigh to Him. Surrender wholly to Him and ask for forgiveness of your sins and commit your illness to Him and your life. Psalm 103:1-5. God bless.

Attention CNN/Access Hollywood: February 19th, 2019-Katy Perry Engagement

Marriage: "Till Death Do Us Part"

Katy Perry recently became engaged to Orlando Bloom. Katy is divorced and is not allowed to marry another man, just as Mr. Bloom is not allowed to marry another woman, for he, too, is divorced. Marriage is "till death do us part."

Romans 7:2-3, reads "A woman who has a husband is bound to her husband as long as he lives, but if the husband dies, she is freed from the law of her husband and is free to remarry." Katy is bound to her first husband. She has to reconcile with him. And Orlando Bloom has to reconcile with his ex-wife.

God Hates Divorce

Further, God hates divorce and has commanded all men, "For what God has joined together, let no man separate," Matthew 19:6.

Divorce-Remarriage Is Adultery

Divorce and remarriage are adultery for, "Whoever divorces his wife and marries another woman commits adultery, and whoever marries her that is divorced from her husband commits adultery."

Likewise, Pink, who is divorced, must reconcile with her husband in order for them to attain their salvation. And even Kate Winslet must be reconciled to her first husband, Jim Threapleton, to attain their salvation. Marriage is "till death do us part."

Apostle Paul said, "To the married, I give this commandment, not I, but the Lord" A wife must not separate from her husband, but if she does, she must remain unmarried or be reconciled to her husband; and a husband must not divorce his wife, 1 Corinthians 7:11.

The Bible clearly forbids divorce and remarriage for those whose former spouses are still living. It is adultery for which there is no salvation. Only if one's spouse dies, then can he/she get remarried. And those who are divorced and remarried with their former spouse still living cannot participate in a Ministry or be members of a Church.

Hollywood stars, work out your salvation through obedience to the Word of God. Do not ignore these alarming Scriptures. Do not think God will make a way for your salvation if you disobey the Scriptures. There is no other way to salvation, except through obeying the Bible. The Bible is the Word of God and it is by His Word that everyone will be judged by whether we obey it or not.

These messages also apply to J. Lo and to Alex Rodriguez who must break off their engagement and reconcile with their former spouses, and to Amazon's Bezos and his wife, who must reconcile, and Jack Osbourne and his wife must reconcile, and also Miley Cyrus and Liam Hemsworth must not divorce but be reconciled.

Ladies, Fragrancenet.com! And don't forget Avon! and Beauty Boutique.org

Let's Get Cooking!
   Coconut Shrimp with Basmati
   Ingredients
   One pound shrimp
   Two eggs
   Bag of shredded coconut
   Oil
   Salt
   Box of basmati rice
   Beat the two eggs, salt. Dip shrimp in eggs and coconut and fry. Boil basmati rice, add butter. You may also add green onion to rice.

   Stuffed Green Peppers
   Ingredients
   Three pounds ground beef
   Two cups rice
   One onion
   Five to six big green peppers
   Salt
   Pepper
   Five bullion cubes
   Tomato paste or can of diced tomatoes
   Cut up one medium onion and fry in oil till browned, add two cups of rice and cover with water and boil until tender. You may have to add more water until rice is tender. Do not boil the rice too tender because it will also cook while boiling in the green peppers with meat. When rice is almost done, throw in the five bullion cubes and wait until they dissolve in the hot rice. Then mix rice in with the beef, salt, and pepper and let sit to cool off. Meanwhile, cut the tops off green peppers and fill with beef meat mixture (you can mix both beef and pork together). You can cut up a tomato and use the slices as lids for the peppers to make sure meat stays in, but it usually stays in without the tomato lids, but a little water can leak in them if they tilt in the pot somehow. Sometimes we may have a little extra space in the

pot, which makes the peppers tilt. If this occurs, you can put the remaining meat mixture between peppers. After securing the peppers, add two tablespoons of tomato paste or a can of diced tomatoes to the water, and boil about twenty to twenty-five minutes until peppers can be easily penetrated with fork, but do not overboil. Plate and serve hot. You may also add sour cream to the meat after opening the pepper in half with a fork or a knife. I like to use beef bullion cubes more than beef broth because they are more flavorful, and the same with chicken bullion cubes, more flavorful than chicken broth. Another way you can stop peppers from tilting is to stand them up in the pot before you stuff them. See how many you can fit in the pot and this is how many you stuff. If you have meat mixture left over, you can still put it in the pot with the peppers. You will just have extra meat to eat. Or you can freeze the remaining meat mixture for later use when you want to make more stuffed green peppers. You are not limited to green peppers. You can use multi-colored peppers: yellow, orange, red, or purple; each one provides a different flavor. Serves six.

Stuffed Cabbages

It is the same recipe as for stuffed green peppers, only you use cabbage instead of green peppers. However, to make cabbage sour, boil it in a pot and add lemon juice to the water. After the cabbage is soft to the fork, you can start pulling away the foils and stuff them with the meat and boil another twenty to twenty-five minutes. Don't forget to add tomato paste to the water in the last twenty minutes of water boiling.

Supa de Galusti-Romanian Grits Soup
Ingredients
Grits
Egg whites from two eggs
Chicken bullion cubes or vegetable flakes or vegeta

In a bowl, beat the two egg whites with a fork until bubbly, do not use a mixer. which will make them cream. Add a pinch of salt. Add a few fists of grits and mix with fork. Add grits until it is thick enough to stay on the spoon. Put a pot of water on stove to boil, then turn down flame. Start adding teaspoons of grits to the water. Do not use a tablespoon because the dumplings will get too big. With a teaspoon, the dumplings grow to almost the size of a fist. Add seasoning: chicken bulluion cubes, vegeta, or vegetable flakes.

Shrimp Scampi
Ingredients
One pound peeled and deveined shrimp
Two cloves garlic
Salt
Garlic powder
Heat oil in pan. Dump shrimp in pan with cut up garlic, salt, and garlic powder. Done when shrimp is pink. Pour oil on shrimp. This eliminates the need for shrimp dip. You can add smoked paprika, Cheyenne (a couple pinches) pepper or red pepper seeds to the pan of shrimp if you want spicy scampi shrimp. You may serve with rice. I usually serve with a side of sour cream or cottage cheese and sautéed pineapple slices. Serves two. For more servings, increase shrimp to two to three pounds.

Shrimp Linguini
Ingredients
One pound shrimp
Garlic powder
Salt
Spaghetti or linguini pasta
Butter
Fry shrimp in pan, add salt and garlic. In a pot, boil the pasta. Drain and add the shrimp and butter.

Romanian Three Story Mussaca
Ingredients
About three pounds of potatoes, medium size
Three pounds ground beef
One medium onion
Can of stewed tomatoes
Salt
Pepper

Cut up peeled potatoes in round slices about a quarter inch wide and put in greased pan. Add the beef mixed with onion, salt, pepper. Then add a row of stewed diced tomatoes. Repeat for a second story. For a third story, add another row of potatoes, beef mixture, and the tomatoes, cover and bake in oven at 400 degrees about twenty-five to thirty minutes. You may add mozzarella cheese between each story. Serve.

Wikipedia: Celine Dion Biography
Who Is Celine Dion?

I found Celine Dion to be a more distinguished star.

Celine Dion (Celine Marie Claudette Dion) was born March 30th, 1968 and is a Canadian singer. Born into a large family from Charlemagne, Quebec, she emerged as a teen star in Homeland with a series of French-language albums during the 1980's. She first gained international recognition by winning both the 1982 Yamaha World Popular Song Festival and the 1988 Eurovision Song Contest, where she represented Switzerland. After learning to speak English, she signed on to Epic Records in the United States. In 1990, Dion released her debut English-language album, Unison, establishing herself as a viable pop artist in North America and other English-speaking areas of the world.

During the 1990's, she achieved world-wide fame after releasing several best-selling English albums such as "Falling In You" (1996), and "Let's Talk About Love" (1997), which were both certified diamond in the US. More international number one hits include: "The Power of Love," "Think Twice," "Because You Loved Me," "It's All Coming Back To

Me Now," "My Heart Will Go On," "I'm Your Angel." Dion's music has been influenced by genres ranging from Rock and R&B to Gospel and Classical. Her recordings are mainly in French and English, although she also sings in Spanish, Italian, German, Latin, Japanese and Mandarin Chinese. She is regarded as one of pop music's most influential voices. She has won five Grammy Awards, including Album of the Year and Record of the Year. Billboard named her the "Queen of Adult Contemporary" for having the most number ones on the radio format for a female artist. She is the second-best female artist in the US during the Nielson Soundscan era. In 2003, she was honored by the International Federation of the Phonographic Industry (IFPI) for selling over fifty million albums in Europe. She remains the best-selling Canadian artist and one of the best-selling artists of all time with record sales of 200 million copies worldwide. Her concert tours and Las Vegas residences have grossed over $1.4 billion, making her one of the most profitable live performers of all time.

Dion was born in Quebec, twenty-four kilometers northeast of Montreal, the youngest of fourteen children of Therese, a homemaker, and Adhemar Dion, a butcher, both of French-Canadian descent. She was raised a Roman Catholic, but a poor, by her account, a happy home in Charlemagne. Music had always been a big part of the Dion family.

Dion cites idols as varied as Aretha Franklin, Charles Aznavour, Carole King, Anne Murray, Barbara Streisand, and the Bee Gees. Celine has expressed admiration for artists, such as Mariah Carey, Whitney Houston, and Madonna, citing they had a profound influence on her vocal style. Her music has been influenced by numerous genres including pop, rock, gospel, R&B, and soul, and her lyrics focus on themes of poverty, world hunger, and spirituality with an emphasis on love and romance. After the birth of her first child, her work increasingly focused on maternal love.

Who would have thought that Celine Dion could sing in eight languages, sell so many copies of her albums, receive so many awards, and come from such a large family, fourteen children in all, that's one more than my family, and she can sing! Her voice is beautiful. So we see why she is a more distinguished star.

Celine, would you like to learn to sing in a ninth language, Romanian? This is my native language. Vine Isus means: Jesus is Coming. This is the title of a Christian song. Will teach you a few more words should you wish to sing with me.

Good Deeds

Hollywood stars donate a lot of money to many good causes and many do other good deeds also. Let's see what the Bible says about good deeds:

1. But do not forget to do good and to share, for with such sacrifices God is well pleased," Hebrews 13:16.
2. And let our people also learn to maintain good works, to meet urgent needs, that they may not be unfruitful," Titus 3:14.

Obey Those Who Rule Over You-Pastors, Ministers, Preachers, and Bible Teachers

"Obey those who rule over you, and be submissive, for they watch out for your souls as those who must give account. Let them do so with joy and not with grief, for that would be unprofitable for you," Hebrews 13:17.

This Scripture refers to those who are called to save souls: Pastors, Ministers, Preachers and Bible Teachers. The Bible further instructs us to, "Let the elders who rule well be counted worthy of double honor, especially those who labor in the Word and Doctrine," 1 Timothy 5:17.

THE DANGER OF ANGERS by Charles Stanley

God expects us to learn to control and not sin. Anger can lead to other sins. When we see the following characteristics in our life, we've crossed the line:

Strife. Proverbs 29:22 says, "An angry man stirs up strife." Although stife can take up many forms, it always pins one person against the other.

Bitterness. Psalm 30:5 says that the Lord's anger is for a moment, and Ephesians 4:26 warns against staying angry overnight. Extended anger festers and eventually leads to bitterness.

Isolation. Whenever anger is nursed, people become isolated from each other. Proverbs 16:28 warns against this by pointing out that "a slanderer separates intimate friends,"

Retaliation. The Word tells us, "Do not repay anyone evil for evil. Be careful to do what is right in the eyes of everyone. If it is possible, as far as it depends on you, live peaceably with all men. Beloved, do not avenge yourselves but rather give place to wrath, for it is written, 'Vengeance is Mine, I will repay,' says the Lord. Therefore, if your enemy is hungry, feed him, if he is thirsty, give him to drink. For in so doing, you will heap coals of fire on his head. Do not be overcome by evil, but rather overcome evil with good," Romans 12:17-21.

Me Too Movement
Lesbian Attack/Coercion
"You won't make it nowhere in stardom unless you go through me.

Me Too Movement
Gang Rape-Met with four men at a hotel for a business discussion, was taken advantage by them, all to my shame.

Me Too Movement
Homosexual Coercions
Men forcing men into sex.

Sex Trafficking
"I, Paul, speak in human terms because of the weaknesses of your flesh. For just as you presented your members as slaves of uncleanness and lawlessness, leading to more lawlessness, so now present your members as slaves of righteousness for holiness," Romans 6:19.

This Scripture means to present your members (your body) as slaves of righteousness. It means not to commit sins including sexual sins anymore but rather use your body for the glory of God.

Wikipedia: Illuminati

1. people claiming to possess special enlightenment or knowledge of something
2. A sect of 16th-Century Spanish heretics who claimed special religious enlightenment
3. A Bavarian sect society founded in 1776, organized like the Freemasons.

*The Illuminati (plural of Latin illuminatus, "enlightened") is a name given to several groups, both real and fictitious. Historically, the name usually refers to the Bavarian Illuminati, an Enlightenment-era society founded on May 1st, 1776. The society's goals were to oppose superstition, obscurantism, religious influence over public life, and abuses of state power. The Illuminati, along with Freemasonry and other secret societies, were outlawed through edict by the Bavarian ruler Charles Theodore with the encouragement of the Catholic Church in 1784, 1785, 1787, and 1790.

The Illuminati incorporate demonic symbols and practices into their worship. Hollywood, steer clear of the Illuminati. Those of you who are members of the Illuminati, you are on Satan's turf, and in the end, will perish into the everlasting fire. Come out, seek God's forgiveness.

The Illuminati see themselves very high and trust in themselves, but Scripture says to "Cast down every imagination and every high thing that exalts itself against the knowledge of God, and bringing into captivity every though to the obedience of Christ," 2 Corinthians 10:5. Further, God is merciful, and "In the past, He overlooked such ignorance, but now He commends all people everywhere to repent," Acts 17:30. God id love and He sent His Son Jesus Christ, who is able to save completely those who come to God through Him because He always lives to intercede for you," Hebrews 7:25.

Quiz

Which is the most read book after the Bible?

It is Annie, the story of a Jewish girl who was captured during the Holocaust after hiding in someone's home for two years and falling in love while in hiding. Did the girl escape the Nazis after being captured by them and marry the man she loved while in hiding? or was she let go by the Nazis, or was she killed by the Nazis? You have to read the book for yourself.

Wikipedia: Angelina Jolie Biography

Angelina Jolie Voight, born June 4th, 1975, is an American actress, film director, screenwriter, an author. She has received an Academy Award, two Screen Actors Guild Awards, and three Golden Globe Awards, and was named Hollywood Highest paid actress by Forbes in 2009, 2011, and 2013. Jolie promotes humanitarian causes and is known for her work with refugees as a Special Envoy and is Goodwill Ambassador for the United Nations High Commissioner fugees. She has often been cited as "the world's most beautiful woman," a title for which she received substantial media attention. Angelina Jolie has been a Goodwill Ambassador for many years and is worthy of recognition for her work.

Angelina has received a Jean Hersholt Humanitarian Award for her humanitarian work and made an honorary Dame Commander of the Order of St. Michael and St. George (DCMG) among other honors. She promotes various causes, including conservation, education, and women's rights, and is most noted for her advocacy on behalf of refugees as a Special Envoy for the United Nations High Commissioner for Refugees (LTNHCR).

Jolie first witnessed the effects of a humanitarian crisis while filming Lara Croft: Tomb Raider (2001) in war-torn Cambodia, an experience she later credited with having brought her a greater understanding of the world. Upon her return home, Jolie contacted the United Nations High Commissioner for Refugees (UNHCR) for information on international trouble spots. To learn more about conditions in these areas, she began visiting refugee camps around the world. In February 2001, she went on her first field visit, an eighteen-day mission in Sierra Leone and Tanzania; she later expressed her shock at what she had witnessed.

In the following months, Jolie returned to Cambodia for two weeks and met with Afghan refugees in Pakistan, where she donated $1 million in response to an international UNHCR emergency appeal, the largest donation UNHCR had ever received from a private individual. She covered all costs related to her missions and shared the same rudimentary working and living conditions as UNHCR field staff on all of her visits. Jolie was named a UNHCR Goodwill Ambassador at UNHCR headquarters in Geneva on August 27th, 2001.

Over the next decade, she went on more than forty field missions, meeting with refugees and internally displaced persons in over thirty countries.

In 2002, when asked what she hoped to accomplish, she said, "Awareness of the plight of these people. I think they should be commended for what they have survived, not looked down upon. Her 2001-2002, her field visits were chronicled in her book, Notes From My Travels, which was published in 2003 in conjunction with the release of her Humanitarian Drama Beyond Borders.

Jolie aimed to visit what she termed "forgotten emergencies" crises that media attention had shifted away from. She became noted for her traveling to war zones, such as Sudan's Darfur region during the Darfur conflict. The Syrian-Iraqi Border during the second Gulf War, where she met privately with US troops and other multi-national forces and the Afghan capital Kabul during the war in Afghanistan, where three aid workers were murdered in the midst of her first visit. To aid her travels, she began taking flying lessons in 2004 with the aim of ferrying aid workers and food suppliers around the world. She now holds a private pilot license with instrument rating and owns a Cirrus SR22 and Cessna 208 Caravan single-engine aircraft.

On April 17th, 2012, after more than a decade of service as UNHRC Goodwill Ambassador, Jolie was promoted to the rank of Special Envoy to High Commissioner Antonio Guterres, the first to take on such a position within the organization. In her expanded role, she was given authority to represent Guterras and UNHCR at the diplomatic level with a focus on major refugee crises. In the months following her promotion, she made her first visit as Special Envoy, her third overall, to Ecuador, where she met with Colombian refugees. And she accompanied Guterras on a week-long tour of Jordan, Lebanon, Turkey, and Iraq to assess the situation of refugees from neighboring Syria. Since then Jolie has gone on at least a dozen field missions around the world to meet with refugees and undertake advocacy on their behalf.

As a public figure, Jolie has been cited as one of the most influential and powerful people in the American Entertainment Industry. For a number of years, she was cited as the world's most beautiful women by various media outlets, and her personal life is subject to wide publicity. She is divorced from her third husband, Brad Pitt, and they have six children, three adopted internationally.

Angelina, I am compelled by Christ to accompany you to refugee locations for the works of the Ministry. This is something I am definitely looking forward to, certainly something for the future.

Crystal Balls/Gazing Balls

Crystal ball gazing involves fortune telling. It is sin. Do not practice such a thing.

Marriage Pet Peeves

Stop leaving your socks on the floor

Don't leave your dirty tissue on the cocktail table

Stop playing that music too loud

Rinse the sink after brushing your teeth

Stop coming home late from work

Stop changing channels while you and your wife watch TV

Please shower daily

Put towel back on rack

Do not have secrets with my children

Don't talk too much with waitresses

Quote:

"Peace I leave with you. My peace I give to you, not as the world gives, do I give to you. Let not your heart be troubled, neither let it be afraid," John 14:27.
Author-Jesus Christ

Catholicism-2nd Commandment Transgressed

"Thou shall not make unto thee any graven image, or any likeness of anything that is in Heaven above, or that is in the earth beneath, or that is in the water under earth. Thou shall not bow down thyself to them, or serve them, for I the Lord thy God am a jealous God, visiting the iniquity of the fathers upon the children unto the third and fourth generation of them that hate Me. And showing mercy unto thousands of them that love Me and keep My Commandments."

Exodus 20:4-6

The Catholic Church has taken out the Second Amendment, but what does Scripture say to those who take out from the Word of God? Scripture says, "If anyone shall take away from the words of the prophecy of this book, God shall take away his part out of the Book of Life, and out of the Holy City, and from the things which are written in this book. So, God will take out their names out of the Book of Life and they will go to Hell forever.

"Any graven image of any likeness that is in Heaven" means Do not make statues of any who are in Heaven, such as God, Jesus Christ, Mother Mary, The Twelve Apostles or any Saints to worship them. Do not bow down in reverence to statues of Heaven beings, such as Statues of Jesus, Mary or the Apostles, as Catholics and other religions do. Do not serve them. This is very detestable to God, and those who practice such things will perish, unless they repent. Hollywood come out of Catholicism. Come out of Buddhism and Hinduism also. Do not serve or bow down to their statues neither.

Spousal Coerced Lovemaking

Hollywood, do not push yourselves on your wives to take you back in bed if she catches you in adultery. This makes matters worse. Give her time to mourn and move past her trauma. Then reunite if she forgives.

Wife, do not be afraid to say, "No, we're not making love. We're going to work on our problem until it is solved." This applies to cheating wives also.

Date Rape

Date rape should not occur, ladies. You are not to be alone with a man. Yeah, this message is outdated, but it's the message of the Lord. If you go out, be accompanied by a male and do not dress provocatively. Also, petting can lead to rape. Some ladies believe they can do petting and not put themselves at risk for date rape. Be wise, ladies. You can prevent many of your rapes.

More Illnesses of Stars

If you are unfortunate to have diabetes as I do, please read.

Wikipedia: Diabetes

Diabetes Mellitus is a group of metabolic disorders characterized by a high blood sugar level. Symptoms of high blood sugar include frenation, increased thirst, and increased hunger. If left untreated, diabetes can cause many complications. Acute complications can include ketoacidosis, hyperosmolar hyperglycemic state, or death. Serious long-term complications include cardiovascular disease stroke, chronic kidney disease, foot ulcers, and damage to the eyes.

Diabetes is due to either the pancreas not producing enough insulin or the cells of the body not responding properly to the insulin produced. Type 2 diabetes is the most common and it begins with insulin resistance, a condition in which cells fail to respond to insulin properly. Signs and symptoms of diabetes include weight loss, increased urination, increased thirst, increased hunger, blurred vision, headache, fatigue, slow healing of cuts, and itchy skin.

Diabetic Diet: Medline Plus

Healthy diabetic eating includes:

Limiting foods that are high in sugar

Eating smaller portions, spread out over the day

Being careful about when and how many carbohydrates you eat

Eating a variety of whole-grain foods, fruits and vegetables everyday

Eating less fat

Limiting your use of alcohol

Using less salt

Please see your doctor before you start any diet or exercise program. Diabetics, invest in a monthly diabetic magazine. It contains many diabetic recipes and articles for diabetics. Google: Diabetic Magazine.

Wikipedia: Diabulimia

Diabulimia is an eating disorder in which people with type 1 diabetes deliberately give themselves less insulin than they need or stop taking it altogether for the purpose of weight loss. Diabulimia is not recognized as a formal diagnosis by the medical or psychiatric communities, but the phrases, "disturbed eating behavior" or "disordered eating behavior" (DEB in both cases) and disordered eating (DE) are quite common in medical and psychiatric literature addressing patients who have type 1 diabetes and manipulate insulin doses to control weight, along with exhibiting bulimic behavior.

Long Term Effects of Bulimia

Severe kidney damage, high blood sugar can overwork the kidneys, leading to kidney failure and the need for a kidney transplant

Severe neuropathy (nerve damage to hands and feet)

Extreme fatigue Edema (during blood sugars controlled phases)

Heart problems

Retinal damage and subsequent vision problems

High cholesterol

Osteoporosis

Death

If you think you have diabetes, go see a doctor.

Wikipedia: Multiple Sclerosis

Multiple Sclerosis is a demyelinating disease in which the insulating covers of nerve cells in the brain and spinal cord are damaged. This damage disrupts the ability of parts of the nervous system to communicate, resulting in a range of signs and symptoms, including physical, mental, and sometimes psychiatric problems. Specific symptoms can include double vision, blindness in one eye, muscle weakness, trouble with sensation or coordination. MS takes several forms, with new symptoms occurring in isolated attacks (relapsing forms) or building up overtime (progressive forms). Between attacks symptoms may disappear completely, however, permanent neurological problems often remain, especially with the advancement of the disease. There is no known cure for multiple sclerosis. Treatments attempt to improve function after an attack and prevent new attacks. dictations used to treat MS, while modestly effective, can have side effects and be poorly tolerated. Physician therapy can help with people's ability to function. Many people pursue alternative treatments, despite a lack of evidence of benefits.

Bible Quiz

The fear of the Lord is the beginning of _____ and the knowledge of the holy is understanding.

Superstition

Ignorance

Wisdom

Answer: Proverb 9:10

Kanye West Converts!

Did you know Kanye West went from Secular Music to Christian Music? Good for him! Kanye also converted having made a confession of his faith in God and that he left his old life behind at the Joel Osteen Church in November 2019. I love to see stars come to faith in Christ. God is awesome!

Wikipedia: Lady Gaga Biography

Stefani Joanne Angelina Germanotta, born March 28th, 1986, known professionally as Lady Gaga, is an American singer, songwriter, and actress. She is known for her unconventionality provocative work and visual experimentation. Gaga began performing as a teenager, singing at open mic nights and acting in school plays. She studied at Collaborative Arts Project 21 through New York University's Tisch School of the Arts.

Gaga is one of the best-selling music artists. She sold twenty-seven million albums and 146 million singles as of January 2016. Her achievements include several Guinness World Records, nine Grammy Awards, and Awards from the Songwriters Hall of Fame and the Council of Fashion Designers of America. She has been declared Billboard's Artist of the Year and Woman of the Year, and included among Forbes' power and earnings rankings. She was ranked number four on the VH1's Greatest Women in Music in 2012 and second on Time's 2011 readers' poll of the most influential people of the past ten years. She is known for her philanthropy and social activism, including her work related to LGBTQ rights and for her non-profit organization, The Born This Way Foundation, which focuses on empowering youth and preventing bullying. Lady Gaga is another highly successful star and who knew that she advocates antibullying concerning youth. Bravo!

Cardi B Awards and Nominations

American rapper Cardi B has many awards, including a Grammy Award, four American Music Awards, seven Billboard Music Awards, four BET Awards, eleven BET Hip Hop Awards, four Art Radio Music

Awards, an MTV European Music Award, four MTV Video Music Awards, three Soul Train Music Awards, and an NR3 Music Award. She has also earned five Guinness World Records during her career.

Rihanna Fenty Beauty

Fenty Beauty is a cosmetics brand launched in September 2017 by singer Rihanna. The

brand is popular for its broad inclusivity across skin tones and gender, especially its Pro Filt'R. The original foundation launch included forty shades, since adding to fifty. The inclusion of Fenty Beauty Concealer includes fifty shades, offering a wide variety to all skin types. The intent behind having so many shades to offer was to differentiate from other make-up companies that didn't cater to a broad market. Fenty Beauty was named one of Time Magazine's best inventions of 2017.

In the brand's first month, Fenty Beauty recorded $72 million in earned media value (a measure of marketing success), ahead of other high-profile brands, including Kylie Cosmetics, Benefit, Urban Decay, KKW Beauty, and NYX. Also, in the brand's first month, Fenty beauty-related content received 132 million views on YouTube.

My Thoughts on Stars

All-time best female singer-Rihanna, followed by late Whitney Houston.

Paris Hilton is one of the most fashionable, best dressed, best hair-styles, best-looking.

Lady Gaga is dressed the wildest, kinda goofy at times.

Selena Gomez is one of the top ten most beautiful females in Hollywood.

Pink looks nice in pink hair, eye-catching.

Christina Aguilera, Paris Hilton and Lindsay Lohan are the least seen in public television.

One of the oddest couples is Blake Shelton and Gwen Stefan, seems Gwen is too wild-looking for Blake.

Hollywood Star: Stop betting all that money saying you're going to get your woman back, but rather put it to good use.

Justin Bieber seems very highly achieved for his young age of twenty-five: very successful in music and married. He has found a wife at a young age.

"He who finds a wife finds a good thing, and obtains the favor of the Lord," Proverb 18:22.

Hollywood Children: Obey Your Parents

"Children, obey your parents in the Lord, for this is right. Honor thy father and mother which is the first commandment, with promise: That it may be well with thee, and that you may live long on the earth," Ephesians 6:1-3.

Fathers, Do Not Provoke Your Children

"And ye fathers, provoke not your children to wrath, but bring them up in the nurture and admonition of the Lord," Ephesians 6:4.

Men Only Section!

This section is only for men. Ladies, please look away, skip this section. Hey, husbands, did you know that wives like to be told they are beautiful even after ten, fifteen, twenty years of marriage. We like to be praised and appreciated more often by our husbands. Wives also love your company, desire to be held by you, to feel loved by you. We are frail and are easily hurt with words or by not paying enough attention to us. Do not tell your wife another woman you see is pretty when you are both out. But instead pay attention to your own wife and tell her she is beautiful. This is the thing to say to her, and in turn, she will bestow more love on you because she feels more love for you. If she feels love emanating from you, she will return that love back. Do practice good hygiene habits, including wearing cologne and good grooming habits. Invest good things in your marriage. Be faithful to your wives, and wives, be faithful to your husbands. Honor and respect one another. Come to the breakfast table groomed and washed and put on a smile. Be joyful. Avoid being grumpy. Had it been bad at the office? Don't let the steam off on your wife. Your wife needs tranquility. She, too, has enough to tend to all day long. She, too, may be exhausted by the end of the day. Can she cook great all the time? Might a culinary class help both of you or find recipes online. Try cooking with your wife once in a while. It is quality time spent together. Take on some of each other's hobbies. So now husbands, go home to your wives and surprise them with the knowledge you know through action. If you already do a lot for your wife, even some of the things in this article, good for both of you.

Husbands and Their Role in Marriage

"Whosoever finds a wife finds a good thing and obtains the favor of the Lord," Proverb 18:22.

"So men ought to love their wives as their own bodies. He that loves his wife loves himself," Ephesians 5:28.

"Husbands, love your wives, even as Christ loved the Church and gave Himself up for it," Ephesians 5:25.

"A soft answer turns away wrath, but grievous words stir up anger," Proverb 15:1.

"Live joyfully with the wife whom you love all the days of the life of thy vanity, which He has given thee under the sun, all the days of the vanity for that is thy portion in this life, and in thy labor which thou take under the sun," Ecclesiastis 9:9.

Ladies Only

Ladies, soak your husband's feet in a nice scented tub of water. It is very relaxing for him at the end of the day. You may even want to add cologne to his feet afterwards. And the husband can reciprocate likewise. Have a candlelight dinner. Play some music. Watch a family friendly movie. Go out to dinner sometimes without the children. Ladies, always be groomed, even early in the morning. Wear your favorite perfumes. Don't let your hair dye wear out nor keep a wardrobe for too long. Wear clothes you know he likes for.

Wives, Marriage, and Love

"The heart of her husband safely trusts in her so that he shall have no need of spoil. She will do him good and not evil all the days of her life," Proverb 31:11-12.

"Wives are to be discreet, chaste, keepers at home, good obedient to their own husbands that the Word of God be not blasphemed," Titus 2:5.

"Wives must be grave, not slanderers, sober, faithful in all things," 1 Timothy 3:11.

"Wives submit yourselves unto your husbands like unto the Lord," Colossians 3:18.

"Be discreet, chaste, keepers at home, good, obedient to their own husbands, that the Word of God be not blasphemed. That aged women be in behavior as becometh holiness, not false accusers, not given to much wine, teachers of good things. That they may teach the young women to be sober, to love their husbands, to love their children," Titus 2:3-5.

Wives Must Submit to Husbands In…Here's examples:
Don't buy this house
Don't invest in this stock
Don't go on this business meeting alone
Don't go out with your friends tonight, you're always gon
Don't wear that dress
Don't go on that vacation
Don't buy this car, buy the one I picked
Don't talk too much
We're not moving to Florida as you wish

We can try to compromise with our husbands, but they get the last word. We are under our husbands. We are not equal with them nor above them. There is a hierarchy:

"God is the Head of Christ, Christ is the head of man and Man is the head of the woman," 1 Corinthians 11:3. Christian wives must obey and honor this hierarchy. Submit in love, try to please your husband. Husbands are our head, means they're in charge. God gave them authority over us, and when we revolt against this authority, we revolt against God, our Father and Creator who gave us breath and who loves us.

Submission to Husband Poem
>Let the husband have the last word
>He is the King of the home
>God gave them power over us
>And authority in which a wife's obedience is a must
>We're in good hands
>God gave them the upper hand
>God gave them the wisdom to lead the home
>You don't do everything on your own
>Your family will not be ashamed
>If the head of the family, to his business he will tend

Wikipedia: Feminism
Feminism is a range of social movements, political movements, and ideologies that aim to define, establish, and achieve the political, economic, personal, and social equality of the sexes. Feminism incorporates the position that societies prioritize the male point of view and that women are treated unfairly within those societies. Efforts to change that include fighting gender stereotypes and seeking to establish educational and professional opportunities for women that are equal to those for men.

Feminist movements have campaigned and continue to campaign for women's rights, including the right to vote, to hold public office, to work, to earn fair wages, equal pay and eliminate the gender pay gap, to own property, to receive education, to enter contracts, to have equal rights within marriage, and to have maternity leave. Feminists also worked to ensure access to legal abortions and social integration and to protect women and girls from rape, sexual harassment, and domestic violence. Changes in dress and acceptable physical activity have often been part of feminine movements.

Being a Pastor and knowing the Scriptures well, feminism has brought revolt against the Bible. Feminists do not want to submit to their husbands anymore as the Bible demands in the above Scriptures. Women detest being told to be keepers at home, which means they should be in the home all the time. However, times have changed, women work outside the home now, but the head is still their husband, 1 Corinthians 11:3, and the wife must still live in submission to her husband and respect him. A Christian wife submits to her husband and respects him.

Me Too Movement

No, sir, I cannot meet with you alone at the hotel. The Me Too Movement told me not to. Can I bring my father, brother, or uncle along?

I believe it is time for women to start being protected again by the men in their lives.

Kwanzaa

Kwanzaa is a week-long annual celebration held in the United States and other nations of the African diaspora in the Americas to honor African heritage in African-American culture. It is observed from December 26th to January 1st, culminating in a gift-giving and a feast. Kwanzaa has seven core principles. It was created by Maulana Karenga and was first celebrated in 1966-1967

American Black Power Activist and Secular Humanist Maulana Karenga, also known as Ronald McKinley Everett, created Kwanza in 1966 as a specifically African-American holiday in a spirit comparable to Juneteenth. The name Kwanza derives from the Swahili phrase "matunda ya kwanza," meaning first fruits of the harvest. Karenga was partially inspired by an account he read of the Zulu Festifal Umkhosi Wokweshwama, which is the annual harvest festival of the Zulu People. This festival has mass participation by young men. There is a black bull sacrifice in the king's hall as the young men work together to kill the animal without weapons.

The Umkhosi Wokweshwama Festival is one of the demonic rituals of Kwanzaa due to the animal sacrifice. Kwanzaa should not be practiced. It is unchristian and should be abolished.

During the early years of Kwanzaa, Karenga said it was meant to be an alternative to Christmas. He believed Jesus was psychotic and Christianity was a "white" religion that black people should shun. Later Karenga withdrew these words, so white people would not be alienated. Now many African-Americans who celebrate Kwanzaa do so in addition to observing Christmas.

Kwanza Principles and Symbols

Seven Principles of Kwanza, which Karenga said is a "communitarian African philosophy."

Umoja-Unity-to strive for and to maintain unity in the family, community, nation and race.

Kujichagulia: Self-Determination-to define and name ourselves as well as to create and speak for ourselves.

Ujima: Collective Work and Responsibility-to build and maintain our community together and make our brothers and sisters problems and to solve them together.

Ujamaa: Cooperative Economics-to build and maintain our own stores, shops and other businesses, and to profit from them together.

Purpose-to make our collective vocation the building and developing of our community in order to restore our people to their traditional greatness.

Kuumba: Creativity-to do always as much as we can, in the way we can, in order to leave our community more beautiful and beneficial than we inherited it.

Imani: Faith-to believe with all our hearts in our people, our parents, our teachers, our leaders, and the righteousness and victory of our struggle.

For each of these principles, there is a candle burnt. These principles promote self-sufficiency and no reliance on God. If these principles do not include faith in Jesus Christ and reliance on Him, they are trash. Do nor wish Happy Kwanzaa to anyone. Doing so makes you a participant in their practices and beliefs. The religion is in itself a segregator.

Did You Know?

Did you know Actress Sarah Jessica Parker is a UNICEF Ambassador? Yes, Sarah was appointed a UNICEF Ambassador in 1997 and has since shown her support in a variety of ways, most notably as a dedicated supporter of Trick or Treat for UNICEF, for which she served as the national spokesperson in 1998, 2003, and 2006.

In June 2011, Sarah Jessica introduced the UNICEF HIV/AIDS Innovation Fund at the Global Business Coalition 10th Anniversary Conference, which was held at Cipriani Wall Street in New York City. She delivered a forceful and moving message to over 300 leading global corporate representatives and other participants about the UNICEF HIV/AIDS Innovation Fund. This fund brings together top HIV experts and diverse business and philanthropic leaders to invest in high-impact, low-cost interventions and technologies that could make an HIV-free generation possible in the future.

"We can accelerate progress against HIV and AIDS and emancipate the next generation from a life burdened by HIV…this is not a choice we have," said Sarah Jessica during her speech, "it is simply what we must do together."

On Mother's Day 2011, Sarah was a signature for an eAppeal encouraging people to purchase UNICEF HIV test kits and help provide rapid HIV tests for mothers to be. Every testing enables HIV positive mothers to take the first step in getting the care they need to resolve their own health and prevent transmission of the virus to their babies. I would like to help Sarah in the case with mothers and HIV.

Sarah Jessica has shown her commitment to the world's most vulnerable children by actively participating in numerous campaigns that support UNICEF's work. From launching the UNICEF Tap Project as the First National Spokesperson for the campaign in March 2007, to lighting the UNICEF Snowflake in New York City in 2004, Sarah has distinguished herself as one of UNICEF's most devoted Ambassadors.

Sarah Parker is also an American actress, producer, and designer. She runs her own production company, Pretty Matches, which has been creating content for HBO and other channels since 2009. She founded the company in 2005 with Alison Benson.

Sarah Parker has become the face of many of the world's biggest fashion brands through her work in a variety of advertising campaigns. In 2000, Sarah hosted the MTV Movie Awards, appearing in fourteen different outfits during the show. In 2003, she signed a deal with Garnier to appear in TV and print advertising, promoting their Nutrisse hair products. In early 2004, Sarah signed a $38 million contract with Gap. Then Parker released her own perfume called Lovely. Later she released her second fragrance "Covet." Then in 2007, she announced her own fashion line, Bitten, in partnership discount clothing chain Steve & Barry's. In 2014, Parker started the SJP Collection, a footwear line at Nordstrom. In 2015, she was named the new spokesmodel for Jordache Jeans. And in April 2018, Parker partnered with Gilt to launch her ready-to-wear bridal collection for modem non-traditional brides. Wikipedia-Biography

Catholicism: Penance

A Sacrament of the Roman Catholic Church that includes contrition, confession of sins to a priest, acceptance of punishment by a Church authority and atonement and absolution, also called reconciliation. It is an act of self-mortification or devotion performed voluntarily to show sorrow for a sin or other wrongdoing.

Penance is when one confesses their sins through a Priest who forgives their sins by God's mercy and grace. They promise to live a more fruitful life through absolution.

The doctrine of penance is false. No Priest on earth has the power to forgive sins. Only God can pardon one's sins. Here are Scriptures which prove God forgives sins:

"If we confess our sins He is faithful and just to forgive us our sins and to cleans us from all unrighteousness," 1 John 1:9.

"For I will be merciful to their unrighteousness, and their sins, and their iniquities I will remember no more," Hebrews 8:12.

"And when ye stand praying, forgive if ye have ought against any; that your Father also which is in heaven may forgive you your trespasses," Mark 11:25.

"As He hung on the cross, Jesus said, 'Father forgive them for they know not what they do,"

"For there is one God and one Mediator between God and man, the Man Christ Jesus e Himself a ransom for all, to be testified in due time," 1 Timothy 2:5-6.

Celebrity Net Worth

Selena Gomez Net Worth: 75 million-singer/songwriter

Ariana Grande Net Worth: 100 million-singer/songwriter

Sarah Parker Net Worth: 150 million-actress/film producer/ fashion designer

Angelina Jolie Net Worth: 100 million-actress/film producer

Adele Net Worth: 175 million-singer/songwriter

Leonardo DiCaprio Net Worth: 260 million-actor/film producer

Justin Bieber Net Worth: 285 million-singer, songwriter

Mariah Carey Net Worth: 300 million/singer/songwriter

Brad Pitt Net Worth: 300 million-film producer/actor

Will Smith Net Worth: 300 million-actor/film producer/rapper

Lady Gaga Net Worth: 320 million-singer/songwriter

Tom Hanks Net Worth: 350 million-actor/producer

Sean Connery Net Worth: 350 million-actor/producer

Serena Williams Net Worth: 350 million- "Queen of the Court." Serena was named

Female Athlete of the Decade.

Mary Kate and Ashley Net Worth: 400 million-actress/fashion designers/businesswomen

Taylor Swift Net Worth: 400 million-singer/songwriter

Rihanna Net Worth: 400 million-singer/songwriter/actress/fashion designer/businesswoman/entrepreneur

Robert DeNiro Net Worth: 300 million-actor

Ellen DeGeneres Net Worth: 490 million-American comedian, television host, actress, writer, producer. Might Ellen DeGeneres wish to convert by coming out of lesbianism for her salvation, so that other women may follow in her footsteps for their redemption?

Beyoncé Net Worth: 500 million-singer/songwriter

George Clooney Net Worth: 500 million-actor/film producer

Elton John Net Worth: 500 million-singer/songwriter

Tom Cruise Net Worth: 570 million-actor

Tyler Perry Net Worth: 600 million-actor/film producer

Jay Z Net Worth: 1 billion-American rapper, song writer, producer, entrepreneur, and record executive. He is regarded as one of the greatest rapper of all times.

Celine Dion Net Worth: 800 million-singer/songwriter

Kardashian Family Net Worth

Kris Jenner: 90 million-an American television personality, entertainment manager, producer, business woman, author

Kim Kardashian West: 350 million-media personality, socialite, model, reality star, and business woman

Kanye West: 250 million-an American rapper, singer, songwriter, record producer, entrepreneur, fashion designer. Kanye's music has spanned a broad range of styles, incorporating an eclectic range of influences including hip hop, soul, baroque pop, electro, indie rock, synthpop, industrial, and gospel.

Kloe Kardashian: 50 million-American media personality, socialite and model

Kourtney Kardashian: 45 million-American media personality, socialite and model

Robert Kardashian: 30 million-American television personality, businessman

Kendal Jenner: 40 million-American model/media personality

Kylie Jenner: 1 billion-American media personality, socialite, businesswoman and model

Caitlyn Jenner: 100 million-American former track and field athlete and current television personality, actress, former Olympian

Celebrity Net Worth by Wikipedia 2019

The Book of Wisdom-Proverbs

"He who covers a transgression (a mistake) seeks love, but he who rep it separates friends," Proverb 17:9.

"As a ring of gold in a swine's mouth, so is the woman who lacks discretion," Proverb 11:22.

"There is one who scatters yet increases more, and there is one who withholds more than is right, but it leads to poverty," Proverb 11:24.

"When the righteous are in authority, the people rejoice, but when a wicked man rules, the people groan," Proverb 29:2.

"Trust in the Lord with all your heart and lean not on your understanding. In all your ways acknowledge Him and He shall direct your paths," Proverb 3:5-6.

Me Too Movement

In the end, what can I say except to be kind one to another. Do not hurt one another. Be merciful and live at peace amongst each other.

Islam

People of Islam can have a better relationship with God through Jesus Christ. Believe in Him, live better, and prosper further for the Lord for He alone is the One who saves, who gives peace and eternal life in Heaven.

Jesus-Only True Savior

Jesus said, "I am the Way, the Truth and the Life. No one comes to the Father except through Me," John 14:6. Further, nor is there salvation in any other name in heaven by which man can be saved," Acts 4:12.

BE YE NOT CONFORMED TO THIS WORLD-Romans 12:2

"Be ye not conformed to this world" means to "not conform to the sins of this world," which include physical appearance, such as wearing make-up, pants, or any provocative clothing. But there are bigger sins we must steer clear of and they are called:

SINS OF THE FLESH

"Now the works of the flesh are evident which are: adultery, fornication, uncleanness, lewdness, idolatry, sorcery, hatred, contentions, jealousies, outbursts of wrath, selfish ambitions, dissensions, heresies, envy, murders, drunkedness, revelries and the like. Those who practice such things will not inherit the Kingdom of God," Galatians 5:19-21. But if you are in Christ, you possess:

THE FRUIT OF THE SPIRIT

"The Fruit of the Spirit is: love, joy, peace, longsuffering, kindness, goodness, faithfulness, gentleness, self-control. Against such there is no law. And those who are Christ's have crucified their flesh with its lusts. If we live in the Spirit, let us also walk in the Spirit," Galatians 5:22-25.

Bible Quiz

The Bible tells us not to boast in ourselves but in

Our achievements

In the cross of the Lord

In the good deeds in the Lord

With peace in our hearts

Answer: Galatians 6:14

Muslims Come Out of Islam

For Jesus said, "I am the Way, the Truth and the Life. No one comes to the Father except through Me," John 14:6.

Catholicism: St. Patrick

St. Patrick was a fifth-century Romano-British Christian Missionary and Bishop in Ireland. Known as the "Apostle of Ireland," he is the primary patron saint of Ireland. He is generated in the Catholic Church, the Anglican Communion, the Lutheran Churches, and the Old Catholic Church, and in the Eastern Orthodox Church as equal-to-the-apostles and Enlightened of Ireland.

Early medieval tradition credited him with being the first Bishop of Armagh and Primate of Ireland, and referred to him as the Founder of Christianity in Ireland, converting a society practicing a form of Celtic polytheism (having many God's). He has been generally regarded so ever since, despite evidence of earlier Christian presence in Ireland.

St. Patrick's Day is observed on March 17th, the supposed day of his death. It is celebrated inside and outside Ireland as a religious and cultural holiday. In the dioceses of Ireland, it is both a solemnity and a holy day of obligation. It is also a celebration of Ireland itself.

Catholicism is not a viable religion. It is a religion emulated from the true Christian faith, which sustains a terribly perverted Gospel by people blinded to the truth as it is written that, "For the time will come when they will not endure sound doctrine, but after their own lusts they will heap to themselves teachers, having itching ears, and they shall turn away their ears from the truth, giving heed to seducing spirits and doctrines of devil's," 2 Timothy 4:3-4.

We are warned that, "We should earnestly contend for the faith for there are certain men who crept in unawares, who were before of old ordained to this condemnation," Jude 1:3-4.

The Gospel of John-The Words of Christ
God Loves the World

"For God so loved the world that He gave His only begotten Son that whosoever believes in Him shall not perish but have everlasting life," John 3:16.

Jesus-Savior of the World

"For God did not send His Son into the world to condemn the world, but that the world through Him might be saved. He who be-

lieves in Him is not condemned, but he who does not believe is condemned already, because he has not believed in the Name of the only
begotten Son of God. And this is the condemnation, that the light has
come into the world and men loved darkness rather than light because
their deeds were evil. For everyone practicing evil hates the light, and
does not come to the light, lest his deeds should be exposed. but he
who does the truth comes to the light, that his deeds may be clearly
seen, that they had been done in God," John 3:17-21.

Jesus-The Living Water

"Whoever drinks of the water that I shall give him will never
thirst. The water that I shall give him will become a fountain of water
springing up into everlasting life," John 4:14.

Jesus Takes Away the Sins of the World

"The next day John saw Jesus coming towards him and said,
Behold, the Lamb of God, who takes away the sins of the world,"
John 1:29.

Jesus Baptizes with The Holy Spirit

"John the Baptist bore witness saying, 'I swathe Spirit descending
from Heaven like a dove and He remained upon Him. I did not know
Him, but He who sent me to baptize with water said to me, 'Upon
whom you see the Spirit descending and remaining on Him, this is He
who baptizes with the Holy Spirit. And I have seen and testified that
this is the Son of God," John 1:32-34.

Worship God in Spirit and in Truth

"God is a Spirit and they that worship Him must worship in Spirit
and in truth," John 4:24.

Jesus-the Judge

"For the Father judges no man, but has committed all judgment
unto His Son, that all men should honor the Son, even as they honor
the Father. He that honors not the Son honors not the Father which
has sent Him," John 5:22.

Jesus-the Bread of Life

"I am the Bread of Life. He that comes to Me shall never hunger and he that believes on Me shall never thirst," John 6:35.

Jesus-the Living Water

"He that believes on Me as the Scripture said, out of His belly shall flow rivers of living water," John 7:38

"If ye continue in My Word, then are ye My disciples indeed, and ye shall know the truth, and the truth shall make you free," John 8:31-32.

Jesus-The Good Shepherd

"I am the good Shepherd, and know My sheep, and am known by Mine. As the Father knoweth Me, even so I know the Father, and I lay down My life for the sheep. And other sheep I have which are not of this fold: them also I shall bring and they shall hear My voice; and there shall be one fold, and one shepherd. Therefore, My Father loves Me, because I lay down My life, that I may take it again. No man takes it from Me, but I lay it down of Myself. I have power to lay it down and I have power to take it again. This commandment have I received of My Father," John 10:14-18.

The Hour Has Come

"The hour has come that the Son of Man shall be glorified. Verily, verily, I say unto you, "Except a corn of wheat fall into the ground and die, it abides alone, but if it dies, it brings forth much fruit. He that loves his life shall lose it, but he that hates his life for My sake shall find it. If any man serves Me, let him follow Me. And where I am, there My servant shall also be. If any man serve Me, him will My Father honor. Now is My soul troubled, and what shall I say? Father, save Me from this hour: but for this cause came I unto this hour. Father, glorify Thy Name. Now is the judgment of this world. Now shall the prince of this world be cast out. And I, if I be lifted up from the earth, I will draw all men unto Me," John 12:23-32.

Walk in Light

Jesus said, "Yet a little while is the light with you, Walk while ye have the light, lest darkness comes upon you, for he that walks in darkness knows not where he goes. While ye have light, believe in the light, that ye may be the children of light," John 12:35-36.

Believe on Jesus

Jesus said, "He that believes on Me, believes not on Me, but on Him that sent Me. And he that sees Me, sees He that sent Me. I am come a light into the world, that whosoever believes on Me shall not abide in darkness. And if any man hears My words and believes not, I judge him not, for I come not to judge the world, but to save the world. He that rejects Me and receives not My words has one that judges him: the word that I have spoken; the same shall judge him in the last day. For I have not spoken of Myself, but the Father which sent Me. He gave me a commandment, what I should say, and what I should speak. And I know that His commandment is life everlasting; whatsoever I speak therefore, even as the Father said unto Me, so I speak," John 12:44-50.

Jesus-A Servant

"Now before the feast of the Passover, when Jesus knew that His hour was come that He should depart out of this world unto His father having which were in the world, He loved them unto the end. After supper had ended, Jesus rose from the table and laid aside His garments, and took a towel and girded himself. After that He poured water into a basin and began to wash the disciples 'feet and to wipe them with the towel with which He was girded. So after He had washed their feet, He sat down and said, 'Know ye what I have done to you. Ye call me Master and Lord, and ye say well, for so I am. If I then, your Lord and Master have washed your feet, ye also ought to wash one another's feet. For I have given you an example, that ye should do as I have done to you. Verily, verily I say unto you, The servant is not greater than his lord, neither he that sent greater than the one who sent him. If ye know these things, happy are ye if ye do them," John 13:1-17.

THE ENDTIMES
Catholicism: Ecumenism
Catholicism is the world's leading religion in the Ecumenical Movement.

Wikipedia: Ecumenism
Ecumenism refers to efforts by Christians of different Church traditions to develop closer relationships and better understandings. The term is also used often to refer to efforts towards the visible and organic unity of different Christian denominations in some form.

The terms ecumenism and ecumenical derive from a Greek word, which means, "the whole inhabited world," and was historically used with specific reference to the Roman Empire. The ecumenical vision comprises both the search for the visible unity of the Church (Ephesians 4:3) and the "whole inhabited earth" (Matthew 24:14) as the concern of all Christians. This is the Wikipedia definition of the Ecumenical Movement, and now I bring my definition of the Ecumenical Movement which is sustained by the Bible.

The Ecumenical Movement is much more, and I am exposing the evil part of it which world powers push for a one world religion are not aware of. I will use the Bible to enlighten readers of this. I will prove that the Ecumenical Movement leads to the end of the world.

Goal of The Ecumenical Movement
The goal of the Ecumenical Movement is to bring the Church back under the control of the Roman Empire as it was at the time Jesus walked on earth and was killed under the Roman Empire, and He will return when the world will again be under the control of the Roman Empire.

The Ecumenical Movement is the religious leg of the coming New World Order, which will bring the world to an end. The New World Order will consist of three parts: A One World Government, A One World Economic System, and a One World Religion (which the Ecumenical Movement will achieve). First let's see what the Roman Empire is.

Wikipedia: The Roman Empire

The Roman Empire was the post-Roman Republic Period of the Ancient Roman civilization, with a government headed by emperors and large territorial holdings around the Mediterranean Sea in Europe, Africa, and Asia. The city of Rome was the largest city in the world.

The Antichrist

The Roman Empire will be led by a future world leader called the Antichrist, who will rise in the end to rule the world for the last seven years before the end of the world and before the Rapture. This seven-year period is called The Great Tribulation. The Antichrist, also called the Lawless Man, whose coming is after the working of Satan will all power and signs and lying wonders, and with all deceit and unrighteousness in them that perish because they did not love the truth, that they might be saved. And for this reason, God shall send them a strong delusion, that they should believe a lie.

"That they all might be damned who believed not the truth, but had pleasure in unrighteousness," 2 Thessalonians 2:8-12.

The Beast Out of The Sea-Revelation 13

The Beast out of the Sea is the Antichrist, a political figure who is given power by Satan to rule the world. Satan is the dragon.

"Then I stood on the sand of the sea and 1 saw a beast rising up out of the sea (this is the Antichrist), having seven heads and ten horns, and on his horns ten crowns, and on his heads a blasphemous name. Now the beast which I saw was like a leopard and his feet were like the feet of a bear, and his mouth like the mouth of a lion. The Dragon (Satan) gave him his power. Let's skip to verse 7 & 8: It was granted to him to make war with the saints and to overcome them. And authority was given him over every tribe, tongue and nation. All who dwell on the earth will worship him, whose names have not been written in the Book of Life of the Lamb slain (Jesus) from the foundation of the world."

The Beast from the Earth

The Antichrist will work hand in hand with the False Prophet, "Then I saw another beast coming up out of the earth and he had two horns like a lamb and spoke like a dragon. He causes all, both small and great, rich and poor, free and slave to receive a mark on their right hand or on their foreheads; and that no one may buy or sell except one who has the mark, or the name of the beast, or the number of the beast which is 666," Revelation 13:16-17.

The Mark of the Beast

The number 666 is called the Mark of the Beast, which will be tattooed in big red numbers, 666, on the head or on the forehead. Anyone who refuses this number will not be able to buy, sell, or trade. This is the economic leg of the New World Order. Those who do not receive this number and worship the beast cannot buy food or sell or trade anything. Those who refuse the number will be killed, although many will escape. This is the One World economic system which will be implemented in the Great Tribulation. It has been revealed to me through visions that the Mark of the Beast will be a tattoo in big red numbers on the hand or on the forehead. Let's see what happens to all who take the Mark of the Beast.

"If anyone worships the beast and his image and receives his mark on his forehead or on his hand, he himself shall drink of the wine of the wrath of God, which is poured full strength into the cup of His indignation. He shall be tormented with fire and brimstone in the presence of the Holy Angels and in the presence of the Lamb who is the Lord Jesus Christ. And the smoke of their torment ascends forever and ever; and they have no rest or night; who worship the beast and his image; and whoever receives the mark of his name," Revelation 14:9-11.

The Great Tribulation

The Great Tribulation is the last seven years before the Rapture. The Great Tribulation will be a very turbulent, frightful, and agonizing time on earth.

Matthew 24 describes it as such, "Therefore when you see the abomination of desolation spoken of by Daniel the Prophet standing in the Holy Place, the Jewish Temple), then let those who are in Judea flee to the mountains. Let him who is on the housetop not go down to take anything out of his house. And let him who is in the field not go to get his clothes. But woe to those who are pregnant and to those who are nursing babies in those days. For there will be great tribulation such as has not been since the beginning of the world until this time, and no, nor ever shall be." You may read the whole Chapter 24. The Great Tribulation ends at The Battle of Armageddon, Revelation 16.

The Rapture

"Behold I tell you a mystery; we shall not all sleep but we shall all be changed, in a moment-in the twinkling of an eye, at the last trumpet. For the trumpet will sound and the dead will be raised incorruptible, and we shall be changed" 1 Corinthians 15:51-52.

Many teach a pre-tribulation rapture, but Revelation. 13;10 tells us that the Tribulation is the patience and faith of the saints-it is the testing of faith. There are more Scriptures which prove that Christians will go through the whole Tribulation and but there is one that stands out and cannot be mistaken.

Let's go to Revelation 7:14-15, "And one of the elders answered saying unto me, 'What are these which are arrayed in white robes and where did they come from?' And I said unto him, Sir thou knowest. And he said to me, "These are they which came out of the Great Tribulation, and have washed their robes and made them white in the blood of the Lamb. Therefore, are they before the throne of God, and serve Him day and night in His temple, and He that sitteth on the throne shall dwell among them."

THE APOCALYPSE
The Seven Seals, Seven Bowls & Seven Judgments
The Seven Seals: Revelation 6:1-17

First Seal

And I saw when the Lord opened the First Seal, and I heard as it were the noise of thunder, one of the four beasts saying come and see. And I saw and beheld a white horse and He that sat on him had a bow, and a crown were given unto Him and He went forth conquering and to conquer.

Second Seal

I had opened the Second Seal, I heard the second beast say come and see. And there went out another horse that was red, and power was given that sat thereon to take peace from the earth and that they should kill one another, and there was given unto him a great sword.

Third Seal

When he opened the Third Seal, I heard the third beast say come and see. And I beheld and it was a black horse, and he that sat on him had a pair of balances in his hand. And a voice said, "A measure of wheat for a penny and three measures of barley for a penny see thou hurt not the oil and the wine."

Fourth Seal

And when he had opened the Fourth Seal, I heard the voice of the fourth beast say come and see. And I looked, and I beheld a pale horse, and his name that sat on him was Death and Hell followed with Him. And power was given unto them over the fourth part of the earth to kill with sword, with hunger with death and with the beasts of the earth.

Fifth Seal

And when He had opened the Fifth Seal, I saw under the altar the souls of them that were slain for the Word of God and for the testimony which they held. And they cried with a loud voice saying, "How long, od, holy and true, doth now not judge and avenge our blood on them that dwell on the earth?" And white robes were given unto every one of them, and it was said unto them that they should rest yet for a little season until their fellow servants also, and their brethren, that should be killed as they were, should be fulfilled.

Sixth Seal

And I beheld had opened the Sixth Seal, and there was a great earthquake, and the sun became black as sackcloth of hair, and the moon became as blood. And the stars of heaven fell unto the earth, even as the fig tree casts her untimely figs when she is shaken of a mighty wind. And the heaven departed as a scroll when it is rolled together and every mountain and island were moved out of their places. And the kings of the earth and the great men, and the rich men and the chief captains, and the mighty men, and every bondman, and every free man, hid themselves in the dens and in the rocks of the mountains. And said to the mountains and rocks, 'Fall on us and hide us from the face of Him that sitteth on the throne and from the wrath of the Lamb. For the great day of His wrath is come, and who shall be able to stand?

Seventh Seal

And when He had opened the Seventh Seal, there was silenced in heaven about the space of half an hour. And I saw the seven angels which stood before God, and to them were given seven trumpets. And another angel came and stood at the altar having a golden censer, and there was given unto him much incense, that he should offer it with the prayers of all saints upon the golden altar which was before the throne. And the smoke of the incense ascended up before God out of the angel's hand. And the angel took the censer and filled it with the fire of the altar, and cast it into the earth; and there were voices and thunderings, and lightenings and an earthquake.

The Seven Judgments: Revelation 8-10

And the seven angels, which had the seven trumpets, prepared themselves to sound:

First Judgment

The first angel sounded and there followed hail and fire mingled with blood, and they were cast upon the earth, and the third part of the trees were burnt up, and all green grass were burnt up.

Second Judgment

The second angel sounded, and as it were a great mountain burning with fire was cast into the sea, and the third part of the sea became blood. And the third part of the creatures which were in the sea and had life: died and the third part of the ships were destroyed.

Third Judgment

And the third angel sounded and there fell a great star from heavening as it were a lamp, and it fell upon the third part of the rivers, and upon the fountains of waters. And the name of the star is called Wormwood. And the third part of the waters became wormwood, and many men died of the waters because they were made bitter.

Fourth Judgment

And the fourth angel sounded and the third part of the sun was smitten, and the third part of the moon, and the third part of the stars, so as the third part of them was darkened, and the day shone not for a third part of it, and the night likewise. And I beheld, and heard an angel flying through the midst of heaven, saying with a loud voice, woe, woe, woe to the inhabiters of the earth by reason of the other voices of the trumpet of the three angels, which were yet to come.

Fifth Judgment

And the fifth angel sounded, and I saw a star falling from heaven unto the earth, and to him was given the key of the bottomless pit. And he opened the bottomless pit, and there arose a smoke out of the pit, as the smoke of a great furnace, and the sun and the aikened by reason of the smoke of the pit. And there came out of the smoke locusts upon the earth and unto them was given power as the scorpions of the earth have power. And it was commanded them that they should not hurt the grass of the earth, neither any green thing, neither any tree, but only those men which have not the seal of God in their foreheads. And to them it was given that they should not kill them, but that they should be tormented five months and their torment was as the torment of a scorpion, when he strikes a man. And in those days shall men seek death a find it, and shall desire to die, and death shall flee from them. And the shapes of the locusts were like horses prepared for battle and on their heads were crowns like gold, and their faces were as the faces of men. And they had hair as the hair of women, and their teeth were as the teeth of lions. And they had breastplates as it were breastplates of iron, and the sound of their wings was as the sound of chariots of many horses running to battle. And they had tails like unto scorpions, and there were stings in their tails, and their power was to hurt men five months. And they had a king over them which is the Angel of the bottomless pit, whose name in the Hebrew tongue is Abadon, but in the Greek tongue, hath his name Apollyon.

Sixth Judgment

And the sixth angel sounded, and I heard a voice from the four horns of the golden altar, which is before God saying to the sixth angel, "Loose the four angels which are bound in the great River Euphrates." And the four angels were loosed to slay the third part of man. And the number of the army of the horsemen were 200 million. And I saw the horses in the vision and them that sat on them having breastplates of fire and of jacinth and brimstone, and the heads of the horses were as the heads of lions, and out of their mouths issued fire and smoke and brimstone. By these three was the third part of man killed: by fire and by the smoke and by the brimstone, which issued out of their mouths. For their power is in their mouth and in their tails, for their tails were unto like serpents, and had heads and with them they do hurt. And the rest of the men, which were not killed by these plagues, yet repented not of the work of their hands, that they should not worship devils and idols of gold and silver, and brass, and stone, and of wood, which neither can hear, see or walk. Neither repented they of their murders, nor of their sorceries, nor of their fornication, nor of their thefts.

Seventh Judgment

And I saw another mighty angel come down from heaven clothed with a cloud, and a rainbow was upon his head, and his face was as it were the sun and his feet as pillars of fire. And he had in his hand a little book, and he set his right foot upon the sea and his left foot on the earth. And cried with a loud voice, as when a lion roareth, and when he had cried, seven thunders uttered their voices.

And when the seven thunders had uttered their voices, I heard a voice from heaven saying unto me, "Seal up these things which the seven thunders uttered and write them not."

The Seven Bowls: Revelation 16:1-21
First Bowl

And I heard a great voice out of the temple saying, "Go your ways, and pour out the vials of the wrath of God upon the earth." And the first went and poured out his vial upon the earth, and there fell a noisesome and grievous sore upon the men which had the mark of the beast, and upon them which worshipped his image.

Second Bowl

The second angel poured out his vial upon the sea and it became as the blood of a dead man and every living soul died in the sea.

Third Bowl

The third angel poured out his vial upon the rivers and fountains of waters, and they became blood.

And I heard the angel of the waters say, "Thou are righteous, oh Lord, which are and was and shall be, because thou hast judged thus.

For they have shed the blood of saints and prophets, and thou has given them blood to drink: for they are worthy."

Fourth Bowl

The fourth angel poured out his vial upon the sun, and power was given unto him to scorch men with fire. And men were scorched with great heat and blasphemed the Name of God, which has power over these plagues, and they repented not to give Him glory.

Fifth Bowl

And the fifth angel poured out his vial upon the seat of the beast, and his kingdom was full of darkness, and they gnawed their tongues in pain. And blasphemed the God of Heaven because of their pains and their sores and repented not of their deeds.

Sixth Bowl

The sixth angel poured out his vial upon the great River Euphrates, and the water was dried up the way of the kings of the east might be prepared. And I saw three unclean spirits like frogs come out of the mouth of the dragon, and out of the mouth of the beast, and out of the mouth of the false prophet. For they are the spirits of devils, working miracles, which go forth unto the kings of the earth and of the whole world, to gather them to the battle of that great day of God Almighty. And he gathered them together into a place called Armageddon.

Seventh Bowl

And the seventh angel poured out his vial into the air, and there came a great voice out of the temple of heaven from the throne, saying, "It is done." And there were voices and thunders and lightnings, and there was a great earthquake such as was not since men were upon the earth, so mighty an earthquake and so great. And the great city was divided in to three parts, and the cities of the nations fell, and great Babylon came into remembrance before God, to give unto her the cup of the wine of the fierceness of His wrath. And every island fled away and the mountains were not found. And there fell upon men a great head out of heaven, every stone about the weight of a talent, and men blasphemed God because of the plague of the hail, for the plague thereof was exceedingly great. The end.

Mel Gibson, let's make these movies about the Seals, Judgments, and Bowls. Let's do the work of the Ministry for the salvation of many. I am gifted with visions. I see into Endtime events through visions. Let's also make a movie of the Antichrist, Revelation 13.